Thanks a Million!

Thanks a Million!

An adventure in biblical evangelism

RAY COMFORT AND KIRK CAMERON

Bridge-Logos

Orlando, Florida 32822

Bridge-Logos

Orlando, FL 32822 USA

Thanks a Million!
by Ray Comfort and Kirk Cameron

Copyright ©2006 by Ray Comfort

Printed in the United States of America.

Library of Congress Catalog Card Number: 2006929483
International Standard Book Number 0-88270-289-0

ACKNOWLEDGMENTS

Our sincere thanks to Jaylene Daugherty,
Anita Alvarado, and Trisha Ramos for their editorial
assistance, and especially to Bev Browning and
Elizabeth Nason for going the extra mile
with this book.

Contents

Preface

In March of 2002, I decided to create a Million Dollar Bill gospel tract. It quickly became my favorite tract because of how well it was received. People loved it. They would laugh, shake my hand, hug me, ask for more, and even begin handing them out to their friends.

By June of 2006, we had sold an incredible 5,700,000. Even our friendly "competitors" were buying them from us and making them available to their customers. Many times I had held them up in churches and conferences and said, "This is not counterfeit, because there's no such thing as a real Million Dollar Bill."

It quickly became Kirk's favorite also, and we not only showed it on our award-winning TV show, but we included it in our Basic Training Course[1] and used it when we did live role-plays at conferences.

Then, on Friday, June 2, 2006, I listened to a voice-mail in disbelief. Our friend, Darrel Rundus, from "The Great News Network"— our sister ministry in Texas, told me that the Secret Service had raided his building and seized more than 8,000 Million Dollar Bill tracts, saying that they were counterfeit.

That night, a Texas news TV cast reported that a "cease and desist" order would be issued by the Secret Service on Monday morning. We had over 700,000 tracts in stock at our ministry in California, and therefore expected a raid from the Feds that day. But it didn't come. That Monday there was a bank-run with panic-buying from customers who loved using the tract. We sold an incredible 500,000 Million Dollar Bill tracts in one day. Our staff was so exhausted that we had to remove it temporarily from our Web site.

Two days later the story hit the *Washington Post*; then it was picked up by the Associated Press and became national news. We ordered over a million and a half of the tracts with the knowledge that if the Secret Service seized them, we stood to lose millions. But as a Christian ministry, we decided to simply render to seizures the things that were Caesar's, and for God the things that were God's. We then would leave it to the courts to decide what belongs to whom.

In case that did happen, we had a reserve inventory of a special print-run of 100,000 copies of the bill with the words, "Secret Service Version" printed in a seal on the bill. This was in compliance with Federal guidelines. Even though it wasn't real money, we made it 1.5 times the size of a genuine bill.

It is my prayer that the Million Dollar Bill tract will not only continue to inspire Christians to share their faith, but it will cause many unsaved people to ask themselves the Million Dollar question—*"Will I go to Heaven?"*

Foreword

This book is an adventure in biblical evangelism. We trust that you are familiar with "The Way of the Master." This is the evangelistic use of the Law of God (the Ten Commandments) to bring the knowledge of sin *before* the Cross is presented. This is what Jesus did, and if you are not familiar with how, when, and why He did it, please see our books, *What Did Jesus Do?* (Genesis Publishing Group) and *The Way of the Master* (Bridge-Logos Publishers).

Admittedly, the principles taught in these books are radically different from those presented by proponents of modern methods. But our challenge to those who care about the salvation of the lost is to be as the Bereans, and take the time to search the Scriptures to see if these things are so. If they are, then we put them into practice and watch what happens. This was the case with the following email we received in May of 2005 in response to "The Way of the Master" TV program:

> Dear Mr. Comfort,
>   You were talking to the guy at the rock concert, and when [he] told you he repents when he sins, you told him (in so many words), "That's of no effect"? God forbid. Straightaway you come off to him as "Holier than thou. Little Goody two shoes." You CAN'T be saying you haven't fallen short since you've been saved,

can you? We all fall short; be realistic! How many times did Christ say to forgive sin, Ray? Was it seven times? Taking a cookie cutter approach to people by repeating the same words over and over to different people makes you sound like a used car salesman laying down his "spiel"...

While that may work great with people sitting in a church who are halfway to the Cross already, you lose your credibility among the ones who need saving the worst ... That's why you're getting so many rejections. You're insulting because you come off so holier than thou ... "I'm Ray Perfect, nice to see you."

(M.G., a Bible student).

We received a further email from him in September of the same year:

Dear Mr. Comfort and Mr. Cameron,

I can't believe it! I used your method of witnessing to one of my best friends, who is an agnostic and by profession a public defender for 30 years. I was nervous at first, but I kept focused on getting to the heart, and not the head ... Ray, I had been trying to witness to people for eight years, mostly "Christ crucified," but it was with limited success. ... Anyway, I feel SO blessed to finally know an effective way to witness to people. I love Jesus, and I love you for showing me the best way to witness to people. Thank you and your whole staff. You are truly doing God's work. ... Thank you so much for showing me how to witness to the "heart and not the head." God bless you all.

In Christ, M.G.
San Rafael, California

P.S. You may have read an email I sent a few months back about my dislikes with your methods. I am very sorry, and have turned 180 degrees since. I thank God for imparting wisdom to you on how to witness properly, and I thank you for telling the world and me.

As you read this book, you will not only see the effectiveness of the Law of God, but you will notice that there is very little use of apologetic arguments like talking to sinners about the subject of evolution, or addressing questions such as, Who made God?, Why is there suffering?, etc. Although we teach how to answer one hundred of the most common questions and also the subject of evolution in other publications (see *The Evidence Bible* and *God Doesn't Believe in Atheists*—Bridge-Logos Publishers), there's a reason why that these issues don't come up. It's because when the Law is used in the way Jesus used it: the conscience is addressed (the place of the knowledge of right and wrong—see Romans 2:15) and not the intellect (the place of intellectual argument—see Romans 8:7). This is what the above email writer meant when he said, "Thank you so much for showing me how to witness to the 'heart and not the head.' This issue and many others are dealt with in great depth in "The Basic Training Course" (see www.WayoftheMaster.com).

May God bless you with and equip you through this exciting publication.

Faithfully in Christ,
Kirk Cameron and Ray Comfort

1

The DTs

by Ray Comfort

A "fishing hole" is a place where the unsaved gather. It's a place for us to share our faith. It could be anywhere, from a stadium parking lot, to outside a movie theater, to a mall, or skateboard park. My old fishing hole was the "Long Beach Town Center." I went there every Friday night for about a year, but stopped going when I began preaching each morning outside the local courthouse. When two members of our staff recently started going to the Town Center, they invited me to join them. Kirk and I were going to team up to go fishing with them, but after considering the battle with Los Angeles traffic, we decided that we would fish in our own spots, and then compare fishing stories.

Have you ever heard of the "DTs"? The letters stand for "Delirium Tremens," and they come as a result of alcohol withdrawal. The DTs cause severe shaking, profuse sweating and paranoia, and produce frightening hallucinations. You will get the DTs (Christian DTs are "Discouraging Thoughts") when you go to your local fishing hole to deliberately share your faith. They will begin the moment you think about going fishing. You will get the sweats, the shakes, and paranoia, and you will have hallucinations of frightening pictures of terrible things to come.

The Bible says that we fight against dark and sinister demonic forces (see Ephesians 6:12). The area of the enemy's attack is our mind. In a sense, we are like unconverted ex-alcoholics. They never see themselves as being free from the disease. Once an alcoholic, always an alcoholic. It's healthy to think like that because it makes them recognize their weakness. They have to understand that they will have a *daily* battle with the temptation to drink alcohol until the moment they die. That's how you and I have to battle the temptation to be paranoid about seeking the lost. Daily.

However, there is a big difference for the Christian. Fear is one of the greatest possessions we have, depending on what we do with it. It can either paralyze or prostrate us. If it paralyzes us and stops us from sharing our faith, it becomes our worst weakness. If it prostrates us before the Lord, crying, "Oh, God, I am so scared. Please help me to stand up for You," then it becomes our strength. It *makes* us trust in God. Our worst weakness then becomes our greatest strength. So always welcome fear to your doorstep, then slam the door of faith in its face. It doesn't need to come into your house. Just having it close at hand will make you pray.

How to Beat the DTs

One great key to personal witnessing is to be resolute. You have to realize that you have an incredibly important agenda, and determine that nothing is going to deter you. You must have the mindset that you are going to have your mind set on seeking the lost. When the DTs come, you will know why they are coming, and you will know how to deal with them. Your weapon is the shield of faith, and its function is to quench all the fearful and fiery darts of the enemy. Faith always overcomes fear. The "fear" that comes to your mind is that if you bring up the things of God, the stranger you have approached will think that you are a religious weirdo. But you know that if he dies in his sins, he will go to Hell forever. Concern for his eternal salvation will help you ignore the DTs. Simply think of this reality—his worst case scenario is the Lake of Fire; yours is that a stranger will think that you are weird. So you *must* make your approach. You are able to do this because you are mentally prepared. That resolute preparation will help you fight off your fears. Your feet have been "shod with the *preparation* of the gospel of peace" (Ephesians 6:15, italics added). Your feet know where they are going because of your preparation. If you are hoping for inspiration without preparation, you may just end up with perspiration.

So, prepare for where you are going to take the conversation. You will greet the person with a warm and courteous, "Did you get one of these?" The "these" to which you are referring are gospel tracts. They are bait for your hook. If you don't have good quality bait, you won't even get a nibble. When you get a bite on your bait, you then have to take control. Quickly pull in the hook with a confident resolve. You know where you want to go, so steer the conversation in that direction. You can do this, with practice. So come with me, and let's do some fishing.

Quality Humor

It's a warm Saturday around 4:00 p.m. in the afternoon. Our fishing hole, Long Beach Town Center, is swirling with activity. There's nothing as exciting for fishermen as seeing the ocean's surface swirling, revealing schools of fish just beneath the surface. Birds above the scene are another indication that fish are present. "Birds" in Scripture are often "types" of the demonic realm. The enemy is ever present when fish are about to be caught.

I walk ahead of our group and see a couple sitting on a bench. I don't hesitate for a moment because hesitation will feed my fears. I have prepared. I know where I am going to go with the conversation, and that gives me comfort.

"Hello. Did you get one of these?"

They don't answer, but each takes a Million Dollar Bill tract. That in itself is an encouragement.

I add, "It's great when you get the change."

They don't smile, so I ask, "Where are you from?"

The woman replies, "Indonesia."

I'm consoled that their lack of evident response to such quality humor isn't personal. It's cultural.

"That's a gospel tract. Have you had a Christian background?"

They both say that they haven't, so I then ask, "Do you ever think about what's going to happen to you after you die? Will you go to Heaven? Do you think that you are good people?"

They both do, so I take them through a few of the Commandments. I ask if they have lied, stolen, blasphemed, and looked with lust. They have. They admit that they are guilty, heading for Hell.

Because there was little verbal interaction, I take them through the gospel and their need of repentance and faith in Jesus. The woman looks at me and says, "We are Buddhists."

I smile and say, "That doesn't matter. Buddhism makes no provision to wash away your sins. Only Jesus can do that."

I thank them for listening and move on. I had the consolation that even though there was little interaction, they had heard the gospel clearly, and that they were both still holding the tracts.

I walked toward three teenagers who where sitting by a fountain. Once again, I took out three Million Dollar Bill tracts, and gave a friendly, "Did you guys get one of these?"

All three refused. That was unusual. So I used my old faithful, "Check the other side."

Curiosity almost always caused a change of mind from someone who initially refuses to take the tract. But that didn't work this time. They totally ignored me. It's frustrating when fish don't bite, especially when you are using *proven* bait. Change of bait. I reached into my pocket and grabbed my faithful "Department of Annoyance" tract.

This looks like a business card, and when someone coldly refuses to take a bill, I follow it up with an official sounding, "This is where I'm from."

Only one responded and took it. But this kid didn't even crack a smile as he looked at the card. That was unusual. I said, "I'm the *director* of the Department of Annoyance."

Still no reaction. I reached for my wallet and did some sleight of hand. That made them smile, so I pointed at the card and said, "That's a gospel tract. Have you guys had Christian backgrounds? Do you ever think about what's going to happen to you after you die?"

I was hoping for some response, and I finally got it. One of them looked at me and earnestly said, "We ... don ... speak English."

The four of us laughed, and I left. It had taken me about three minutes to figure out that the lake in which I had been trying to fish was frozen solid, and that was the reason for the cold response. I wasn't discouraged that my icebreakers didn't work, because even seeming failures add to our experience. Besides, failures are relative.

The Worst

My worst failure happened years ago on one dark Friday night in Santa Monica. It was worse than when, as a new Christian, I knocked on a door, aware that Jehovah's Witnesses had stolen our evangelistic thunder when it came to going door-to-door.

When it opened, I said to the woman who opened it, "Hello. I'm not a Jehovah's Witness." She said, "Well, I am!"

It was worse than when I was trying to witness to two young women, and asked the pregnant one a friendly, "When are you due?" She said, "I'm not!"

Santa Monica was worse than both of those incidents and every other failure I have had combined.

It was a dark Friday night. I had been open-air preaching, and in between sessions I was giving tracts to folks who passed by when I saw a sight that broke my heart. A woman, crippled from some terrible disease, was in a motorized wheelchair and heading in my direction. She was moving so fast I didn't even have a chance to hand her a tract, and felt disappointed.

However, a few minutes later I was delighted to see her coming back. This time the wheelchair was being pushed by another woman, which meant that it was moving slower and I therefore would have a chance to hand her a tract.

As they approached, I politely reached out to give a tract to the poor woman. She reached out to take it, but the disease had twisted her hand and caused it to flail about so that she couldn't take it. She looked so disappointed that I decided to walk alongside her and help her take it. The second attempt failed. Her twisted hand thrust back and forth like a gasping fish out of water. Her facial expression revealed her frustration. I resolutely followed the hand with the tract. Still she couldn't grab it. Back and forth we went as I walked with them. The more I attempted to help her take hold of it, the more her muscles made her frustrated hand thrash back and forth, something evidenced by her facial expression. Suddenly, the lady pushing the chair said, "*Can't you see she doesn't want it?*" Duh. Super-duh!

The poor lady hadn't been trying to grab it. *She had been trying to push it away!* The frustration on her face wasn't there because she wanted the tract and couldn't take hold of it. It was there because some nut case with a stupid piece of paper wouldn't get out of her face. As I stood there, I felt like bowing my head and quietly praying, "Lord, if You are thinking of taking me home sometime in the near future, now would be a really good time."

So you can now see why speaking for three minutes to three kids who didn't speak English didn't discourage me. Failures are relative.

Back to Long Beach. I spotted a couple sitting down with a young child. It was then that I suddenly got an attack of the DTs. In came the sweats, the shakes, and the hallucinations. They were vivid and came with Surround Sound: "This woman may be open to the gospel, but her husband certainly won't be. He is buff, which means that he works out. His body is his god. He is puffed up with pride and therefore hates religion, and he particularly hates stupid religious fanatics who try to push their own narrow-minded brand of religion down people's throats (and chase people in wheelchairs). Besides, the little kid with them is a sure sign that it will be a nightmare to try and start any means of communication. The kid will definitely interrupt, wanting things, and perhaps even screaming loudly and making the whole attempt completely futile. I should just turn around and go home."

I refused to change my course, because my feet were shod with preparation. I approached the couple, handing each of them a Million Dollar Bill and giving my usual spiel. She was friendly. He looked at me suspiciously. I said, "It's a gospel tract. Do you have a Christian background?"

He said, "We're Mormons." Back came the DTs: "These were Latter Day Saints. They were schooled in their religion. Rich, educated folks. They are ready with a thousand powerful arguments about the true way of salvation: Mormonism."

I took no notice, and asked, "Do you consider yourself to be good people? Do you think that you will go to Heaven?" They both did, so we went through the Commandments into Grace.

"Are you two married?"

They weren't.

"Are you living together?"

They were. So I politely but firmly said, "That's fornication. And the Bible says that no fornicator will go to Heaven. If you died right now you would both end up in Hell."

I paused and then said, "Thank you so much for listening to me. This is so important."

The woman looked at me and earnestly said, "*I know it.*"

I told them that they needed to repent, trust in Jesus as they would trust a parachute to save them, and then read the Bible and obey it. They both seemed to be appreciative that I had taken the time to talk to them. I shook their hands and left.

Next I saw three youths sitting at a table at an outdoor restaurant. More DTs: "You can't just walk up and start talking to people who are sitting at a table. What are you going to do next—sit down with them? That's the epitome of impertinence."

Have you ever noticed what waitresses do when people are talking at a table on which they are waiting? They don't wait for a gap in the conversation. They butt in and say, "Are you ready to order?" Do their patrons get upset? Of course not. She's there for their benefit. She has an agenda. She's bold because she knows that she has what they want. Food.

Here's a good tip. We have what the world wants. They just don't know it yet. We know it, so we can be bold. With God's help, we can make them hunger for righteousness. We have an agenda. They may think you're a little strange at first, but experience will teach you that you can do it.

I politely butted in on the three youths' conversation. "Did you guys get one of these? It's a million dollars[2]. Cool huh?"

They smiled as they took one each.

"Would you like to see a bit of magic?"

They nodded, so I turned two one dollars into five. That impressed them. I pointed at the tracts and said, "Those are gospel tracts. Have you guys had Christian backgrounds?"

They had.

"Do you consider yourselves to be good people?" They did. We went through the Commandments. They listened intently, understood that they were guilty and that if they died that day, they would go to Hell.

I shared the gospel and then added, "You know, guys, I have a lovely wife and a nice house. I would rather be there right now. But I'm not. This is because I care about you and where you will spend eternity. So please think about these things seriously."

Their facial expressions showed me that they understood what I was saying. I shook their hands and left.

The experience reminded me of when my associate, Mark Spence, and I were nearly kicked out of a restaurant in Chicago. The pizzas we ordered seemed to take an eternity to be brought to our table, so Mark and I excused ourselves and walked around the dozen or so tables, handed out Michael Jordan collectible tracts and did "The Light Show"[3] for each table. The patrons loved it. They were even asking us to sit down and join them at their tables.

As we turned around to go back to our own table, we were stopped by the manager and a big bouncer. The manager sternly asked, "What do you think you are doing?"

I managed a smile and said, "We gave out some free Michael Jordan collectibles and were showing people our light show."

He wasn't impressed. He said, "I want you to leave right now!"

"Our *whole* party?"

He looked a little taken aback. "Your whole party?"

"Yes. There are ten of us. We're here with the local pastor and his elders. I'm their guest speaker."

Suddenly we were more than welcome to stay. He didn't want to upset the local pastor. That may have upset the local church. And that may have upset his local income.

My final Long Beach fishing session happened when I saw another three teenagers heading my way. Hoping they spoke English, I resolutely stepped in front of them and said, "Did you guys get your million?" They each grabbed one.

"Wanna see some magic?" They did. They were very impressed.

"Those are gospel tracts. Do you have Christian backgrounds?" They were Catholics. I ignored the DTs about Mary, the pope, confession, purgatory, transubstantiation, etc., and instead asked if they considered themselves to be good people. They did, and after going through the Law, one asked, "But what about asking for forgiveness?" I told them that wouldn't help them. They needed to repent and trust in Jesus alone for their salvation. They were very sober.

"You're young guys, and you're surrounded by sexual temptations. Get your hearts right with God because you don't know when you are going to die."

I told them that 150,000 people die every twenty-four hours, and that there was nothing more important than their eternal salvation. Afterwards they were upbeat and seemed to appreciate my concern for them.

Our team (made up of two members of my staff—Anna and Dale Jackson—and three of their friends) then met in a well-known coffee shop, and we compared fishing stories. We spoke about trying to fish on ice. The ones that got away. Nibbles and bites. And of course, the DTs.

2

Electric Evangelism

by Kirk Cameron

I recently had a professional electrician do some wiring in my house. I knew I wanted to witness to him, so I planned my approach. It started with prayer. "Lord, please prepare this man's heart and help me open my mouth boldly as I ought to." I said to the electrician, "Good morning. How are you doing?"

"Good. You?"

"Great. Thanks for doing such a great job on my house. I really appreciate it."

"Yeah, no problem."

"Can I ask you a question? Have you ever gotten shocked doing your job?"

"Oh, yeah ... (laugh). A few times. It doesn't feel good!"

"Have you ever gotten shocked really bad ... like almost died?"

"Yep. One time I grabbed the wrong wires and I felt the jolt go right through my chest and I couldn't move. It was scary."

"Have you ever known anyone who's died from a shock like that?"

"Yeah, one time on a job, I heard a guy scream from up on the roof. We ran to see what happened and there he was slumped over a transformer box—dead."

"Wow. You have a really dangerous job. Do you pray before you go to work each day? Because maybe you should."

"Yeah, I do sometimes."

"Really? That's cool. I was an atheist most of my life, but now I really love God. You know what did it for me? The Ten Commandments."

"How so?"

"Well, would you consider yourself to be a good person?"

We had a wonderful conversation. I walked him through the Law (as we often demonstrate on our TV program) to show him that according to God's high standards, neither he nor I was a truly "good" person. He readily admitted to breaking all of the Commandments. I then asked him to recall his friend and think back about how harsh the consequences were for violating the law of electricity.

"If you think about it, God has created many laws—the law of gravity, the law of electricity, and the law of light. None of them bends. And there is a law that is stronger than all of these—God's moral Law. It's written on your heart so that you'll know right from wrong. Isn't that true?

"Yeah."

"Listen to what the harsh consequences are for violating that Law. The Bible says, 'all liars will have their part in the Lake of Fire.' 'No thief, and no adulterer will inherit the Kingdom of Heaven.' So does that mean that if you were to die today, you'd go to Heaven or Hell?"

"Hell."

Because the man was obviously concerned about the subject matter, I shared the gospel with him. Then I said, "Do you know what God did for you so you wouldn't have to go to Hell? Do you know what He did to show you His love for you?"

"No. Tell me."

"For God so loved the world that He gave His only begotten Son ..."

I explained to him that God was "not willing that any should perish, but that all should come to repentance." We talked about the Cross where Jesus died to pay the price for the sins he has committed against God, and that if he will repent and trust in the Savior, he could be forgiven and transformed by the Holy Spirit of God, and given eternal life. I asked him, "So when do you think you'll get things right with God?"

"Really soon."

"Isn't it possible you could die on your next job, or even on this one?"

"Absolutely."

"Then please don't let too much time go by. Just find a quiet place and cry out to God. Ask Him to forgive you for your sins, and decide to turn away from them once and for all. Willfully put your faith in Jesus Christ to save you and He will. God will never let you down. May I pray for you right now?"

"Sure."

We prayed together; he thanked me for our deep talk and was grateful when I gave him *The Evidence Bible* and a copy of *Save Yourself Some Pain*. I encouraged him to read it every day and find a good church. The expression on his face looked like something between shock and delight at the uniqueness of the morning's events. I was privately praising God for His faithfulness to both of us.

So the next time you find yourself with an opportunity like this, find a way to open up a friendly conversation about life and death, Heaven and Hell, repentance and faith. I'm telling you, it's electric!

3

Be Careful
What You Pray

by Ray Comfort

B e careful what you say to God. Experience has taught me
that He often answers a prayer, even if it's mumbled. One
day I muttered, "Lord, I know I have been preaching the gospel
every day to groups of unsaved people, but I really need to do
some one-to-one."

Later that day, I was in our call center when I noticed two
temporary signs for our ministry. We had them made while we
were waiting on a permit to create a special "Living Waters
Publications" sign incorporated into a waterfall.

I grabbed the signs off the table and decided I would tie
one of them to the back gates of the ministry, so that at least
delivery drivers would know that they were in the right location.
I didn't realize that our ministry manager had asked one of the
employees to hang the signs.

As I picked them up, Danny (the employee) asked a friendly,
"What are you doing with those signs?" I was his boss, so I
just smiled, put them behind my back as I walked away and
said, "These are the signs that follow those who believe."

As I tied the sign to the fence, a man across the alley called
out, "What's that? Living Waters?"

"It's a publishing company."

"Oh."

As I was about to tie it to the gate, two obvious gang members walked down the alley. I said, "Hey, guys, did you get one of these?" I quickly grabbed two tracts from my pocket and handed them one each. As they read the tracts, I said, "They're Christian tracts. Have you had a Christian background?"

One of them answered, "No."

I asked for their names and tried to log them into my memory.

"What do you think happens after someone dies?"

"I haven't thought about it much."

"Where are *you* going?"

"Heaven, I hope."

I then went through almost exactly the same wording as with Fred, and walked them back to the lobby to give them "What Hollywood Believes" CDs, as they didn't read books.

"What are your names again?" (I should have been wearing Jon's T-shirt.)

They then told me their names (again), and I said, "Those are unusual names."

"Yeah. They're gang names."

"Can you remember my name?"

"Keith?"

"No, it's 'Ray.'"

I spotted EZ, our manager, as we entered the lobby, so I called him over and introduced him, explaining that he used to be a gang member. After EZ shared his testimony with them, I gave them some material and said, "If someone puts a gun to your head and pulls the trigger, it means Hell forever. Can we pray for you guys?"

The talkative one said, "Sure. Pray for this homeboy."

I did pray for them, thanking God that they were open, asking that He would remind them of their sins against Him, and give them understanding about what we had spoken about.

I then went outside, finished hanging the sign, and walked back into the lobby. While I had been witnessing to the gang members, I noticed two people talking to my wife in the packing room. One was an attractive blonde; the other was a gentleman in his early twenties. As I entered the building, he was seated in the lobby.

"Hi, I'm Ray. What's your name?"

"Ryan. I'm from Pitney-Bowes. I was just checking your postage machine."

"Did you get a free book?"

"No."

"Oh. I'll get you one. It's called *What Hollywood Believes*. Have you had a Christian background?"

"No."

"What do you think happens after someone dies? Do you believe in Heaven and Hell?"

"No. You just die."

"Are you an atheist?"

"Yes, I am, actually."

"See this building? How do you know there was a builder? Isn't the building proof that there was a builder, even though you have never seen him?"

"Yeah ..."

"Same with a painting and a painter. The painting is proof that there was a painter. When you look at creation, that proves there was a Creator."

Amazingly, Ryan nodded in agreement and quietly mumbled something about the complexity of life forms.

"Do you consider yourself to be a good person?"

He did, but as I was about to take him through the Law, the door opened and the blonde returned from the restroom. That made the situation a little awkward, so I gave her a book, signed it, and asked, "Do you have a Christian background?"

"I was raised a Mormon, and have just started going back to church."

I didn't want to get into a debate about Mormonism, so I explained to her (I've forgotten her name) that I was talking to Ryan about a test to see if he was good enough to get into Heaven. "Listen in. It's interesting. Ryan, there are four simple questions. Are you ready?"

He nodded.

"Have you ever told a lie?"

After we went through the Law, Ryan admitted that if God judged him by the Ten Commandments, he would end up in Hell.

"Does that concern you?"

"Not until I talked with you."

I then took him through the Cross, repentance, and faith, talked about the importance of getting right with God that day, and they were on their way.

Wow! I thought about how, in thirty minutes, I had witnessed to six people face-to-face, and how faithful God is to bring prepared people to us if we are prepared to speak to them.

Then I remembered what I had in my pocket. It was a new tract that read: "Here's my phone number. Give me a call the day you are going to die, and we will talk further about eternity." It brought home the truth that we don't know when we are going to die, so we had better make peace with God today. I should have given each of these six people one of those tracts! I consoled myself by mumbling, "Never mind. There will be other times."

4

Divine Appointments

by Kirk Cameron

I was walking from my car to the front door of our ministry offices when I noticed a man in a black jacket on a moped scooter, driving through the adjacent alley with three dogs. He stopped in front of one of the office windows and peered inside. When he realized I was watching him, he said, "Excuse me. What kind of business is this?"

"A Christian ministry" I told him. I thought this might be a good witnessing opportunity, so I bent down and struck up a conversation with his dogs whose names were Tiger, Sarah, and Samson. After the pooches and I talked doggie talk for a while, the man (whose name was also "Kirk") said, "Hey, you look like *that guy!*" He told me how he had seen me recently on television talking about God and asked, "What made you go *that way?*"

I shared my story of being an atheist turned Christian and asked him to tell me his story. He unloaded his whole story on me almost as if he needed someone to talk to.

He told me that he was married, but had lost his job. He told me he had been using cocaine and loved to smoke marijuana. He had lots of guns at home and had recently tried to commit suicide by hanging himself with a chain in his garage.

He said, however, that he wasn't "strong enough" to go through with it and only put his head through the homemade chain noose to see what it would feel like. I gulped.

This guy was really nice. He was polite and had a smile on his face. To look at him, you wouldn't know anything was wrong. I asked him if he believed in God.

He said, "Sure I do." The rest of our conversation went like this:

"What do you think happens when you die?"

"I'm not sure."

"Well, would you consider yourself a good person?"

"Yes, I think so."

"Do you think you've kept the Ten Commandments?"

"Probably not."

"Well, I can take you through a few of them and you can see how you're doing. Is that OK?"

"Sure."

Have you ever lied?"

"Oh, yes. Many times."

"What does that make you?"

"A liar."

"Have you ever stolen anything, no matter how much it cost?"

"Yes, I have, and that makes me a thief."

"Right. Jesus said, 'Whoever looks upon a woman to lust after her has committed adultery with her …'"

"Oh, yes, I've committed adultery many, *many* times."

The tone of his voice changed and he dropped his head, resting his chin against his chest. He was suddenly quiet. I continued.

"Sir, you just admitted to being a lying thief and an adulterer, and you've got to face God on Judgment Day. If God judges you according to the Ten Commandments, do you think you'll be innocent or guilty?"

"Guilty."

"So does that mean Heaven or Hell?"

"Hell."

From this point on in our conversation, he was very contemplative. It was apparent to me that this man knew that he was in trouble with God. We talked about the seriousness of sinning against a Holy God and the reality of God's just punishment. He didn't argue or try to make up excuses. I discerned that conviction was upon him and he was ready for Grace.

We talked for another half hour about God's love for him and how God demonstrated it by sending His only begotten Son to die for him on the Cross, making a way for him to be reconciled to his Creator. I explained repentance and faith, and he seemed to have a very good grasp on what those words meant. He didn't try to complicate things or offer up excuses for his past actions, but said he understood that the only thing he felt he could do was to stop doing those things and ask God for help. I reemphasized the necessity of dying to himself (not to end his life by hanging from a noose, but to live for God) and trusting in Jesus Christ alone to save him from sin and lead him as Lord.

The man's eyes welled up with tears as we continued to talk. I gave him some things to help him along in his spiritual journey (a "Soundly Saved" CD and Save Yourself Some Pain booklet) and asked him if he'd like to pray. He was very grateful and we prayed together in the alleyway.

He told me about how a relative of his had turned to God because of a miraculous event in his life and how he wished that God would do something out of the ordinary for him as some sort of a "sign." I laughed as I thought about how out of the ordinary it was for a man named Kirk to happen to ride his moped by a Christian ministry building at just the moment "that guy" (another Kirk) was walking into that same building, to strike up a conversation about God which clearly shows him "the way," and to end up praying together for salvation. I asked him if he thought our meeting could possibly be the sign he was looking for. He looked up to the heavens, smiled, and then nodded his head and said, "Maybe it is." He gave me a hug and his business card, and said he'd be back one day.

As he rode his moped down the street with Tiger, Sarah, and Samson following behind, I prayed for him and thought about how wonderful God is to arrange such divine appointments in such unexpected places.

> *Where can I go from Your spirit?*
> *Or where can I flee from Your presence?*
> *If I ascend into Heaven, You are there:*
> *If I make my bed in Hell, behold, You are there.*
> *If I take the wings of the morning,*
> *And dwell in the uttermost parts of the sea;*
> *Even there Your hand shall lead me,*
> *And Your right hand shall hold me (Psalm 139:7-10).*

5

Ear Pressure

by Ray Comfort

When Kirk and I boarded a flight from Los Angeles to Alabama, I sat next to a young man named Chancey, who was on his way to Ohio from Hawaii. He took the "red-eye" and was asleep for the first hour of the flight. On his lap, I noticed a book, which gave me insight into what he was studying—political science. When he awoke, I immediately began to ask him about himself. He was very friendly and despite having just woken up, seemed to enjoy the conversation.

After some time talking with me, he asked, "Where are you two going?"

I told him that Kirk was speaking at a church that night, and asked, "Have you had a Christian background?"

He had. He was an Episcopalian. I asked him if he thought about his death very often. He did, and said that he had been thinking of becoming a chaplain, and that he sometimes wondered if he had enough faith.

I said, "You know what helped me get the whole issue straight? It was one question. Let me give you a quick test—it will really help you. Do you consider yourself to be a good person?"

His answer was perceptive, "I think everybody does. Everyone justifies whatever actions they do."

Here goes the test. "Have you ever told a lie?"

He had. He had also stolen, blasphemed, and looked with lust.

"Chancey, listen to this: by your own admission, you are a lying, thieving adulterer at heart, and you have to face God on Judgment Day. If He judges you by the Ten Commandments, will you be innocent or guilty?"

"Guilty."

"Would you go to Heaven or Hell?"

"I would go to Hell."

When I asked him if it concerned him, he said, "What do you mean?"

I told him that he should be *horrified* at the thought of going to Hell for eternity. He was concerned, so I explained the Cross to him, and then I encountered something frustrating. He said that he had been confirmed about a year previous to our conversation, and that it was then that he was made right with God. Yet it was evident that he wasn't saved. When under the light of the moral Law, he was guilty and heading for Hell, yet unbelievably, he was taking consolation in his religious traditions.

I asked him again, "If you died right now, where would you go?"

"I would go to Hell."

"Then your confirmation was meaningless when it comes to your salvation."

He agreed.

A moment later he began to study the book on his lap. I said, "Chancey, I'm going to ask you the same question again before the end of this flight. If you died right now where would you go?"

"Hell."

I decided at that point to give him some ear pressure. "Isn't that amazing? Here you are, admitting that if this plane crashed, you would end up in Hell forever, and all you do is read your book. You should be aghast. If we both stand before God on Judgment Day, and you are still in your sins, and you see me separated to Heaven and you end up in Hell, you will demand, 'Ray, why didn't you slap my face?' I can't do that to you because it would offend you. All I can do is slap you with words. I don't want your money. I'm not saying to join a church. Examine my motives. I simply care about you and where you spend eternity. There should be sweat dripping from your brow."

Chancey was an "awakened" sinner, but he wasn't "alarmed." You will find these people often. They admit that they have sinned, that they are on their way to Hell, but their concern isn't great enough for them to do anything about it. All you can do is give them literature, lovingly slap them with words, and then pray with them—if they will let you, and for them after you part. I did that with Chancey.

Have you ever turned on the cold water in your home and heard a family member scream from the shower? There are repercussions for your actions. Sin is like that. There are repercussions for its actions. When we put our hand to sin, usually someone along the line is going to get burned. When we lie, someone is getting burned. When we steal or commit adultery, someone is getting burned. However, there are times when we sin where no one gets burned. When we lust, covet, hate, or blaspheme, it doesn't hurt anybody. *That's why it's so important to emphasize that all sin is against God.* When David committed adultery, he cried out to God, "Against You and You only have I sinned." It is *His* Law that is being violated, and because of that we are the ones that are in hot water with God.

How to Stop Religious Nuts

I was sitting on a plane, flying back from Alabama. Kirk was across the aisle from me. We planned to do some work together on a new book called, *The Way of the Master for Kids*, but we couldn't get seats together. Sometimes things didn't work out the way we plan. That's the wonderful thing about being a Christian. We always have the consolation of Romans 8:28. I could see that Kirk was witnessing to the young man sitting next to him, and it was obvious by his facial expression that he was open to what Kirk was saying.

The name of the man sitting next to me was Mike. He was reasonably friendly as I asked him about himself. He lived in Charlotte, North Carolina, and he was on his way to California to interview for a new job. As I spoke to him, I was hoping that he would ask me what I did for a job, so that I could bring up the things of God. He didn't ask, so I said, "I write Christian books. Have you had a Christian background?

He said, "No. I only got two hours sleep, so I'm going to get some shut-eye." He then put his seat back, closed his eyes … and closed my mouth.

Two hours later, when he awoke, I said, "So, you are not at all concerned about your eternal salvation?"

He looked at me and said, "I only discuss religion and politics with my family."

I smiled and said, "May I join your family?"

He simply said, "No."

I was more saddened than discouraged. This man probably felt a smug sense of satisfaction in that he had a pat phrase to get rid of religious nuts. What a tragedy.

Another reason I wasn't discouraged was that two days earlier I had preached open-air in the rain to about thirty people who lined up outside the local courthouse. Most of them had umbrellas, and as soon as I mentioned the things of God, a gentleman standing directly in front of me turned his back (and his umbrella) toward me. Many times I had preached to the backs of people, but I could at least see the backs of their ears and felt that the sound had a chance of reaching them. But preaching to a big black umbrella was discouraging. It was a tragedy beyond words that the man was using an umbrella to shelter himself from the gospel that told him how he could be sheltered from the terrible rain of God's wrath.

But there is a biblically evangelistic philosophy by which each of us should live. It is, "Jesus was despised and rejected by men." That's the bottom line. If we live for Him, we too will be despised and rejected by men. Anything on top of that is a bonus. When He fed multitudes and healed the sick, they loved Him. But when He spoke of sin, righteousness, and judgment, they hated Him. Jesus said that He spoke of the world's evil deeds and that's why He was hated. He also said that if they had hated Him, then they will hate us. When you and I do what Jesus did, we shouldn't be surprised to get what Jesus got.

When we arrived at Los Angeles International Airport, I handed a tract to a woman and her two kids. When I detected an accent, I asked where they were from. They were Australians who had just arrived in the United States. About ten minutes later, the woman approached me and frantically asked how to get a shuttle to Terminal Four. Kirk and I were being picked up, so we said that we could all squeeze into our car and drop them at Terminal Four.

That's what we did. Four of us squeezed into the back seat. It was very cozy. I knew that I had between one and two minutes to witness to them. The thought entered my mind that I had given them tracts and a "What Hollywood Believes" CD (which had a very comprehensive gospel presentation). But what if they didn't listen to it and they died on their flight? I had no choice. I had to be faithful. I swallowed my fears and gave them the thumbnail version of the gospel, and they were out of the door in about two minutes.

Memos From Hell

If you decide to share your faith, be ready to get a "memo from Hell." The word "memo" comes from "memorandum." According to the dictionary, it is "a written proposal or reminder." Your boss will give you a memo telling you what he wants you to do. It's his will for you to fulfill.

If you have enlisted in the Christian faith, you have begun a new job. The Bible is now your memo. It is there to inform you of your new Boss's will. When you were in the world, you had a different boss. His memos dictated your lusts. You joyfully ran to do his will. You once served sin, but you quit because you suddenly discovered that there was going to be a payday, and you didn't like the wages. They were gross. The wages of sin is death. A down payment had already been dealt to you in this life, and full payment would have come in Hell in the next. It was a real bad deal. Thank God that you had the good sense to obey His command to quit before payday came.

However, your old boss is a sore loser. He didn't like having to let you go. He desperately wants you back, and he keeps bugging you with memos. These are special messages that are designed to discourage you from working for your new Boss. These are *personal* dictates formulated for you by subtle satanic secretaries, who know what to send you. They usually play on your fears and your weaknesses. These personal memos will usually be delivered to you through the mouth or pen of some individual from whom you least expect it. And they will come at just the right time to do their dirty demonic work.

I will never forget my first personalized memo. It came way back in 1974. I was about to preach open-air for the first time in my life. I was terrified, but I had determined to preach. I was gathering courage while looking at about twenty to thirty people who were sitting on some steps in the local square of my hometown. Another Christian came alongside me, unaware of what I was planning to do. He looked in the same direction and casually said, "Look at that bunch of people. Hardly worth preaching the gospel to them," and walked off.

It was perfect timing. Too perfect. I realized what was happening, ignored the memo, and preached anyway. I thank God that I opened my mouth that day, because I ended up going back to preach open-air at that location more than three thousand times. If I had listened to the memo, I might never have gone back there again.

Perhaps you would like to preach open-air, but you are a woman. The moment you let your desire be known, get ready for a memo. Someone will tell you that it's not a woman's place to preach. So let me give you my thoughts on the subject. I think the Scriptures are very clear about the place of women within the Church. From my understanding, women holding a place of spiritual leadership (authority over men) within the Church is unbiblical. However, I don't see any biblical grounds for the Great Commission being restricted to the male gender. When Jesus said to pray for laborers, I don't think He meant men only, and most within the Body of Christ would agree with me that *every* Christian, male *and* female, is commanded to preach the gospel to every creature. The Apostle Paul certainly involved women in the task of evangelism. He said "And I urge you also, true companion, help these women who labored with me in the gospel, with Clement also, and the rest of my fellow workers, whose names are in the Book of Life" (Philippians 4:3). Women "labored" with him "in the gospel."

So it is therefore at least biblically sound for a woman to preach one-to-one. How about one-to-two? What happens if a woman is sharing the gospel and four people or more gather around? Is one-to-fifteen okay? Think of the woman at the well. The Bible says "The woman then left her water pot, and went her way into the city, and said to the men, Come, see a man, which told me all things that ever I did: is not this the Christ?" (John 4:28, 29). When she told the men, "Come see a

and wrote an email back to tell him how important it is that we use the Law to draw people to Christ.

No doubt other memos will come. They are signs that we're doing the right thing for the Kingdom of God. If we're not getting attacked, it would mean that we're not being effective for the Lord.

So, if you're going to seek and save the lost, you too should be ready for that "personalized" memo. When it comes, tell the deliverer that he can take it back to where it came from. He can get behind you, because you are no longer your own. Christ bought you with a price. You would never think of quitting. The benefits are too great. Then set yourself to work at the job God has called you to do—to be a fisher of men.

6

David and Goliath

by Ray Comfort

I would rather preach to ten thousand angry machete-wielding atheists than talk to my relatives about the things of God. They scare me. This is because if a stranger becomes upset with me, he may call me a fanatic and walk off. It's not a pleasant experience, but I've lost nothing except my dignity. I can handle that. However, if I offend someone I deeply love and *they* walk off, I lose a relationship.

My nephew, David, and his live-in girlfriend were visiting the States and spending the day with us before their flight left for Australia that night. I asked my son-in-law to say grace and peeped at our guests to see how they reacted to the prayer. David opened and closed his eyes as though he wasn't sure what to do. Jenny kept her eyes open the whole time, which told me something about her attitude toward spirituality. My discerning mind told me that this was a sign that she hated Christians. She also hated the Church. I discerned that she was a God-hating atheist. The moment I poured fuel onto her by mentioning spiritual things, she was going to burst into uncontrolled rage. It was a David and Goliath situation.

Then I thought of how to bring the subject of spirituality up. "The Way of the Master" TV program was on just after lunch, so I invited them to sit with us and watch it. They did. In silence. There was no reaction at all. None.

After the program, we decided that I would drop them at a local mall for a final shopping spree. I planned to speak to David about his salvation in my van. I had to. It could be the last time I would ever see him, and I couldn't live with myself if I didn't care enough to talk to him. I was encouraged to see that he got into the passenger seat and Jenny got into the back. Tackling them individually would make it easier. Here goes ...

"David, I appreciate your watching the program with us. Do you ever think about what happens after you die?"

"Not much."

I gave a little of my testimony and said that life didn't make sense to me if death could snatch the ones I loved or me at any moment. It was an awkward conversation and didn't really go anywhere, and this was David—the one who *closed* his eyes. Goliath was sitting in the back seat and didn't hear our conversation.

Suddenly we were at the mall. I decided that I would run at Goliath and if I was killed and my flesh fed to the birds, so be it. I picked them up a couple of hours later.

When I picked them up, I suggested visiting another store miles away. That would give me more time.

"Jenny, I was talking to David about his spiritual beliefs. Do you ever think about what's going to happen to you after you die?"

"Not much."

"Not at all? Have you ever lost someone you love?" She said that her grandmother had died.

"Didn't that make you think about death, and what happens to people? Something in you should say, 'I don't want to die!' Your will to live should kick in."

David nodded a little. That encouraged me.

"Don't you realize that you are either going to be murdered, die in an accident, or die from disease? Jenny, are you an atheist?" She said that she wasn't and that she believed in God. So much for my discernment.

"David, do you believe in God?"

"Sometimes I do and sometimes I don't."

I then explained that he could know God existed because of creation. The building is proof that there was a builder, the painting is proof that there was a painter, and creation is absolute proof that there was and is a Creator. He nodded. More encouragement.

"Do you think that you will go to Heaven if there is one?"

Jenny said, "I hope so."

"Are you good people?"

Both of them said that they were, so I asked if I could give them a little test to see if that was true. David gave hesitant permission.

"Have you ever told a lie?" They had.

"Ever stolen?" They had.

"Ever used God's name in vain?" They had.

I looked at David and said, "This one will nail you. It did with me. Jesus said, 'Whoever looks upon a woman to lust after her has committed adultery already with her in his heart.' Have you ever looked upon a woman and lusted after her?"

"Yes."

I looked back at Jenny and asked if she had broken that Commandment. She had.

"Listen to this. By your own admission, both of you are lying, thieving, blasphemous adulterers at heart, and you have to face God on Judgment Day. If He judges you by the Ten Commandments, will you be innocent or guilty?"

"Guilty."

"Will you go to Heaven or Hell?"

David looked taken aback. He said, "Hell."

I asked if it concerned him that if God was to judge him by the Ten Commandments, then he would end up in Hell for eternity. He said that it did. I began to tell them what Jesus did on the Cross for them—that He paid the fine so that they could leave the courtroom. I explained that this life is a holding cell with a big blue roof, good lighting, and good air conditioning, but that it was a holding cell because the Judge of the Universe had proclaimed the death sentence upon humanity. He said, "The soul that sins, it shall die."

I said that through Jesus, God could commute our death sentence, that we are free to go if we do what the Bible tells us to—repent and trust the Savior. I explained that repentance means turning from sin, and that faith in Jesus is more than just a belief. It is a trust—the same way you trust yourself to a parachute. Then I casually asked, "Did you see *The Passion of the Christ?*"

They said that they had. That surprised me. Australia isn't like America. Generally, Australia is not as open as America to the things of God. I joyfully explained that the brutality of the movie reflected the truth of the Bible. Jesus was more marred than any man, so that we could go free from God's wrath. I thanked them both for listening to me and told them how nervous I was for fear of offending people I love. They smiled. Goliath was actually Zacchaeus. That night I gave both of them copies of the pocket version of *The Evidence Bible*, and after they left, we had a time of special prayer for them, thanking God for the opportunity to speak to them and for His faithfulness to continue to grow the seed planted that day.

The Elderly Woman

On a plane to Chicago I sat next to an elderly woman named Jean. I gave her a book, and an hour or so later said that I was going to speak in a church the next morning.

I asked, "Do you have a Christian background?"

"It depends what you mean by Christian."

"Are you born again? Do you know what that means?"

She leaned close to me and said, "I have God in my heart."

As she leaned towards me, her face seemed to change, and I suddenly felt that I was talking directly to a demon. She looked evil. It was as though there was a stubborn, proud, condescending, and mocking spirit speaking to me.

I asked, "Do you believe in Heaven and Hell?"

She didn't, but with a little coaxing, she let me take her through the Good Test. I was able to get her permission to do so by saying that these questions really helped me.

She said, "You can't judge where I'm going to go."

I agreed, and said that the four questions would help her judge for herself. She had nothing to lose. She gave me permission, and we began to go through the Commandments. The Law stirs up a hornet's nest of justification.

"You can't tell me that God is not going to allow me into Heaven because I stole an orange as a child."

After reasoning with her about idolatry and how I had made a god to suit myself, and how if God is good, He must be just, she retreated to saying, "I will never be born again. Never."

I said, "What do you mean by born again? Tell me what you think it means."

She couldn't give a definition, but told me that she knew people who were "born again" that she liked as individuals, but then spent the next fifteen minutes telling me how they said one thing and then did another: lying, dishonest deals, and oppressing their wives. She said that one of her bosses once told her something she would never forget. He said, "Never trust anyone with dirty fingernails. And never trust anyone who tries to convert you."

I said, "I agree with you. There's a lot of bad stuff out there. Just watch Christian television. So much of it is horrible."

She smiled as though I was conceding, that she was totally justified in what she said. I continued, "But it's the same with certain races. You can't judge the whole race simply because there are some bad ones among them."

It was as though she suddenly saw that she was as guilty as someone who was racially prejudice. I put my hand on hers and said, "I appreciate you listening to me."

She smiled and returned the gesture. I didn't press the issue any further because I knew that she had begun reading *What Hollywood Believes* and had put it in her bag, and I would pray for her that night.

When the flight ended, she said, "Good luck with your talk tomorrow." Then she reached out and gently touched my arm, and said, "I enjoyed talking with you."

7

Kimo Therapy

by Ray Comfort

I was standing in a long line at the Los Angeles airport when I saw an elderly gentleman wearing a missions uniform and holding a box. It had "Aging Veterans" written on it. As I got closer to him, I found myself resenting the fact that he was standing there, begging. My initial thoughts weren't very loving.

Then I looked at the man and began to think, "He's elderly himself. Standing there when most people are probably resenting his waving a collection box under their noses. Why is he doing it? Perhaps he's unsaved and afraid of dying, and this is his way of doing something good. He wants to go to Heaven. The poor man. He's deceived by self-righteousness."

I leaned forward and warmly asked, "Do people give very often?"

He answered in a very kind tone that made me want to hug him. "Some people give very generously."

"Are you a Christian?"

"Oh, yes. I was brought up in a Christian home."

"Are you born again?"

"No, I'm not. I've only been born once."

He answered in a spirit of humility, so I gave him a "What Hollywood Believes" CD and said that it would help him. Then

I handed him a coin with the Ten Commandments on one side and the gospel on the other. He was very grateful, and said, "The Ten Commandments. I like that."

The Different Voices

Tune into Christian television and you will hear what is said to be in God's will. He speaks to many preachers. So they say. God tells them what sweater to wear, what to say when, and about who and why. These are the "God told me" folks. However, any pastor or ministry/church leader worth his salt will immediately send up his antenna when he hears "God told me" terminology.

If you and I feel that we have God's leading, it is wiser to say, "I think that I have God's leading in this." Of course there are many Bible verses about hearing His voice, but there's a big problem when someone maintains that God personally "spoke" to him about doing or saying something. In essence he is saying, "I'm not open to your input. I don't care about or want to hear what you have to say. What I'm doing is what *God* wants. I don't need your wisdom. It's God's way (my way) or the highway." It closes the door to godly counsel, and that can easily be perceived as being manipulative.

It is such a serious thing to say that we have had Almighty God speak to us, because it is close to saying, "Thus saith the Lord," and in the Old Testament, getting that wrong was a death sentence. More than likely, this type of talk often comes more from the circles in which we have moved, rather than from insincerity.

Over the years, I have seen examples of earnest Christians saying, "God told me," and they proved to be wrong. Two couples maintained that God told them that they were having baby boys. Both had girls. One earnest young man contacted me, adamant that God had told him that there was going to be an earthquake in the Seattle area. This guy was no flake. He was sincere and concerned that if someone didn't alert authorities, many lives could be lost. So that's what he did. He went to the media and humbly told them that God had warned him of an impending earthquake and that the people needed to be warned. There was no earthquake.

We have a number of "voices" with which to contend. First, there is the subconscious. It continually speaks to us. It's the voice that won't let you sleep at night when you have had a problem during the day. It works like a long chain that links one thought with another. It's the voice that rarely stops. It feeds your mind with thoughts day in and day out. What's more, it's very difficult to control. Try telling yourself that you'll turn it off. You are not going to think of anything. You'll find that it'll still talk to you like a dripping tap.

Second, there is the voice of your conscience. That's a voice that we don't really like hearing. It tells us when we infringe the Moral Law. Its moral voice is such a reality that even an atheist has difficulty in denying it. He cannot refute the fact that there is a voice that speaks to him about his morality. When he lies or steals, it makes its voice heard, irrespective of his will.

Third, there is the voice of the spiritual realm that we battle. The Christian who goes to share his faith with a stranger knows this subtle voice. It will tell him that he can't speak to a stranger, that he will make a fool of himself. It can be a voice of discouragement or it can be the voice of sexual seduction, whispering unclean thoughts to a sinful heart. It can come as a voice of pride, as a dark sinister voice, or as the voice of a gentle angel of light, but its source is "spiritual wickedness in high places."

It is because of these different voices accessing our complex minds that we need to exercise godly discernment. The way to do that is to weigh every thought with the Word of God. If love isn't the reason for the voice you are hearing, then cast the thought down. Look at Scripture:

"Casting down imaginations, and every high thing that exalts itself against the knowledge of God, and bringing into captivity every thought to the obedience of Christ ... " (2 Corinthians 10:5).

The Greek word used for "imaginations" is *logismos* and, according to *Vine's Expository Dictionary*, is "suggestive of evil intent, not of mere reasonings."

You Made My Day

The man walked into one of our offices. He was sturdy in build, probably in his mid-twenties. He had arrived at our new building to put together two desks. As he walked toward me, I said, "Hi. Have you come to do the desks?"

"Yes, sir."

"What's your name?"

"Kimo. What's yours?"

"I'm Ray. Do you get sick of your work?"

"No. I kind of like it actually. I get to go to new places each day."

As he stood looking at the unopened boxes, I said, "I write Christian books. Have you had a Christian background?"

"Yes, sir."

"Are you born again?"

"No."

"Do you know what it means?" I asked.

"Yes. It's when you accept Jesus Christ as Lord and Savior."

"Do you consider yourself to be a good person?"

"I'm a great person," he replied.

"May I ask you a few questions to see if that's so? I will give you the Good Test. Are you ready?"

"Yeah."

"Have you ever told a lie?"

"Yes."

"What does that make you?"

"What do you mean?" he said.

"If I lied to you, what would you call me?"

"A liar." He looked back at his instructions for putting the desk together.

"Just give me thirty seconds."

He put the instructions down and gave me his full attention. Kimo turned out to be a lying, thieving, blasphemous adulterer at heart, but when I asked him where he would go if God judged him by the Ten Commandments on Judgment Day, he said that he would go to Heaven, because he asked God for forgiveness. When I used the civil law analogy to show him that it wouldn't help him, he ran behind the thin bush of self-righteousness. He said that he did good for people. I took him back to civil law and explained that no judge would begin to listen to a devious criminal boast about what a good person he was because he did good things. That flushed him out into the open. His mouth was stopped.

I then took him back to civil law and explained about someone else paying the fine for a criminal, and how the judge would let him go, not because he was sorry or that he wouldn't do it again, but because the fine had been paid. I then explained the blood of the Cross, and that Kimo's fine was paid in full, and that the way to access that payment was through repentance.

I said, "Kimo, if you died right now, you would go to Hell. God would give you justice. Do you have a Bible at home?"

"Yes, I do."

"Let's pray. Father, I thank you that Kimo has been so open to listen. I pray that You speak to him further about his eternal salvation, and his need to repent and trust Jesus as Lord and Savior. I pray Your blessing on him and his family. Please keep them in health. In Jesus' name, Amen."

"Amen." Kimo said. Then he stepped forward, stretched out his hand toward mine, shook it enthusiastically, and said, "You pretty much made my day with this."

Angry Ernie

I witnessed to a big truck driver once. His truck was big. Really big. Somehow his name suited him. Ernie. He and his wife smoked liked trains, and traveled along with their dog in the cab. It was a beautiful border collie—the smartest of dogs. Ernie was at our ministry, unloading a huge shipment of books.

During the unloading, I slid alongside him and said, "They are Christian books. Have you had a Christian background?"

He said that he hadn't. It turned out that even though he considered himself to be a good person, he had broken almost all of the Commandments.

I looked at him and asked, "Do you think you will go to Heaven or Hell?"

"Heaven."

I gently told him that he wouldn't get in because he had sinned against God. Then I asked him if it concerned him that he would end up in Hell. He said that it didn't concern him at all.

"Ernie! You should be terrified. The Bible says that Hell is a place of eternal torment."

He stepped back; his expression changed to one of anger. He looked directly at me and said, "I kicked a friend out of my home for preaching at me. I may just get in my truck and leave!"

He was fuming.

"Ernie, I'm sorry if I offended you."

I went quiet for a moment and said, "I teach Christians how to share their faith inoffensively. You know, Ernie, it's very unusual for someone to get offended with that approach; perhaps one in a thousand. Most people understand that I care about them. I don't want your money. I'm not saying that you should join my church. I'm just concerned for you. It took a lot of courage on my part to speak to you like this. Can you give me thirty seconds to tell you what God did for you?"

"Okay."

I then shared the Cross with him. He then opened up to me about how both his mother and father had died.

A short while later, his wife came around the corner. I said, "I've been talking to Ernie about the things of God." She smiled and said that she had been trying to encourage him into that direction for years. I gave them a book and a CD. They both let me pray for them, and afterwards, Ernie asked me for my phone number because he wanted to keep in touch.

How true it is: "He that rebukes a man afterwards shall find more favor than he that flatters with the tongue."

May I Have a Million?

Later that week I wasat a banquet in Dallas, Texas. As I entered a plane to fly back to Los Angeles, I handed a Million Dollar Bill tract to a flight attendant at the door. She loved it, so I gave her one for each of the pilots. Both of them responded with laughter. That attracted the attention of one or two passengers, so I asked, "Did you get yours?" and gave about a dozen out as I made my way to my seat.

A few minutes later one of the flight attendants approached me and said, "May I have a Million Dollar Bill for a man in the front?" I handed her six or seven, saying that she could have as many as she wanted. She held them up and said out loud to the rest of the other passengers, "Who wants a million dollars?" Immediately she began handing them out to outstretched hands. It was obvious that I hadn't given her enough, so I grabbed a handful from my pocket and tossed them over the back of my seat to folks behind me. Later on in the flight I felt a tap on my shoulder, and looked up to see a lady pointing at my pocket, saying, "May I have a million?"

I can't tell you what a delight it is to use this tract to reach out to the lost. I have often said that even if it didn't have a gospel message on it, it would be a blessing to give it to people because it makes them so happy. Their smiles make me smile. But this little piece of paper carries the message of everlasting life to dying humanity, so how much more should we take advantage of its effectiveness? Don't let a fear of rejection stop you. Simply formulate different phrases in your mind that you feel comfortable with as you pass them out, and in time your confidence will grow. You could use my favorite—"Here's your million dollars ... it's great when you get the change." Or "You're doing a good job." I have even dropped them out of my car window (don't do this on the freeway), and watched with delight as two youths circled around on their bikes and picked them up off the not-busy street. Or simply leave it with someone who has just sold you something or done you a service, and say, "Thanks a million."

8

Open-air at a Public High School

by Kirk Cameron

I have a friend named Joey who loves people, and therefore shares the gospel with them. He has a unique approach with strangers. He calls it "iPod evangelism." He walks up to people with his iPod in hand and asks them if they would like to do an audio interview for a new Web site. Most are very willing and agree to let him record them. He begins with the question, "If you saw a human and a cat drowning in a swimming pool, which would you save first?" Most all say, "The human, of course." Then Joey asks, "Why?" This question leads into a statement of values and world-view, and opens the door for Joey to say, "That's interesting. Is that because you believe in God or something?"

By this point, people are deep in thought about what they believe and why, and Joey walks them through the fact that we all have to die. He talks about the issues of sin, righteousness, judgment, and grace, and encourages them to get right with God as soon as possible. He then posts the interviews for us all to listen to on his Web site (all with the interviewee's permission). I love going to his site, listening to his uncensored witnessing encounters. You will too! Check it out at www.AdventuresInChristianity.com

Recently Joey had another unique idea. He invited me to a local public high school to open-air preach. He assured me that the principal was a Christian and had given us permission to have our meeting. We arrived just before lunch, signed in at the office, and set up our box of tools (a small stand containing copies of *The Evidence Bible* and *Save Yourself Some Pain* booklets) in the pool area just as the school had instructed us. As soon as the bell rang, Joey and I (along with some Christian students) spread the word about the meeting. We passed out Million Dollar Bills to as many kids as we could and then I saw an opportunity. The majority of students were hanging around the cafeteria tables, eating and dancing where a DJ was playing some tunes. I asked the Rhyme Master if Mike Seaver could say a quick word to the kids, and he turned down the music and handed me the mike. With a few dollar bills in my other hand, I jumped onto a tabletop (missing someone's lunch by a foot) and said over the loudspeakers, "Excuse me, my name's Kirk and we're having a meeting at the pool in about five minutes. We're going to be talking about God and money and will even be giving away some free real money for anyone who can answer some trivia questions for me. So grab your lunches and come with me."

Just at that moment, I hear a loud male voice behind me say, "Get down from there! You can't do that!" I turned to see a very serious looking man with dark sunglasses, pointing his finger at me. I quickly got down from the table and said quietly, "Sir, I believe I have the principal's permission to do this." With an even louder voice, he said, "I *am* the principal!"

I felt myself shrink a few inches as I tried to apologize for the misunderstanding. Apparently he thought I was staging the meeting right there in the cafeteria instead of having it in the pool area on the other side of campus. I tried to explain that I was only letting the students know where to meet us, but he cut me off and said sharply, "Just give me that microphone and go to the pool!" I thanked him for his kindness and trotted off to the pool with lots of kids following me. When I arrived, there were about one hundred and fifty students waiting for the meeting to start.

I began by giving away real dollar bills to anyone who could answer trivia questions about money, like "What is the root of all evil?" and "What wouldn't you do for one million dollars?" I then switched to the subject of God and offered $20 to anyone who could pass the "Good Person" test. The students were clamoring for the chance to pass the test and go home $20 richer. I told them it was a four-question test:

1. Have you ever told a lie?
2. Have you ever stolen anything (regardless of the value)?
3. Have you ever looked with lust (which God sees as adultery of the heart)
4. Have you ever used God's name in vain (blasphemy)?

Of course, no one proved to be a truly "good" person (only Jesus could do that), but all the students were quiet, respectful, and listening to the open-air discussion. I shared with the crowd that no one (including me) is "good" according to God's standards (see Romans 3:10), and that we are all guilty and in desperate need of His forgiveness. I explained that the Cross was God's demonstration of His great love toward us "in that while we were yet sinners, Christ died for us," and that Jesus rose from the grave to conquer death and the power of sin. I pleaded with them to repent and trust in the Savior, Jesus Christ so that they could find eternal life.

A few great questions came from the crowd, and I did my best to answer them, always trying to point them back to the Cross. When the lunch bell rang, about thirty kids came forward wanting Bibles and answers to more questions. Joey and I hung around for another hour talking and praying with seeking students. It was wonderful to see what God did that day with the principal's permission.

Todd: Well, she should know what this is all about, right?

Aaron: Pretty much.

Todd: Or does she not have her cards with her?

Aaron: Oh, I … she's just sitting on the couch watching television. I don't know why. She knows what's going to happen anyway.

Todd: You're at the beach. She's on a couch watching television and it's … Are you getting hosed down? What's happening?

Ray: This is California, dude.

Aaron: (inaudible)

Todd: So, it's Amy, correct?

Aaron: Yes. It's Amy. Let me run into the shop—the psychic-reading shop, and you can take it. Take it from there.

Host: Oh, good, he's going into the psychic shop.

Aaron: Up. Up. Here she is.

Todd: Is she going to charge us for this? Okay, Ray, you talk to her.

Amy: Hello?

Ray: Hello, Amy?

Amy: Yes, hi …

Ray: How are you doing?

Amy: I'm doing fine. I'm Amy from Psychic Boutique in Newport Beach Peninsula.

Ray: How long have you been a psychic, Amy?

Amy: Forty years.

Ray: Forty! You don't sound like you're forty. So, you've been one since you were a baby?

Amy: No, not completely.

Ray: And how did you know you had these psychic abilities?

Amy: Oh, even my mom does this, and my grandmother.

Ray: A generational thing.

Amy: I'm a third generation psychic.

Ray: And how do you know that what you're getting is genuine?

Amy: Well, because people tell me it's true. Sometimes people walk in; I can tell them their names, their dates of birth, the situations they're involved with. You pick up their energy, okay.

Ray: Yeah, their spirit? Is that what you're saying? … Amy, can you give me your thoughts on what happens after somebody dies?

Amy: You're asking me if there is a Heaven?

Ray: Yeah, I'd like to know your thoughts.

Amy: Yeah, definitely there's a Heaven.

Ray: There is?

Amy: Definitely. There's a Heaven.

Ray: Where'd you get that from? Is it from the Bible?

Amy: … Yes, it's from the Bible … I am religious.

Ray: So what sort of background … what religious background do you have?

Amy: Protestant. I'm Protestant.

Ray: Oh, you are?!

Amy: Mmm.

Ray: Okay. So, who goes to Heaven?

Amy: All the good people go to Heaven, okay.

Ray: Where do the bad people go?

Amy: The bad people go to Heaven too. Okay.

Ray: They do?

Amy: It makes it more difficult for them.

Ray: So, it's not just good people that go to Heaven. It's bad people.

Amy: All people go to Heaven, one way or another.

Ray: Do you think there's a Hell?

Amy: You know, they say *this* is Hell. What we're living in now.

Ray: Are you having an enjoyable life?

Amy: Yes, I am.

Ray: Then it can't be Hell then, can it, if you're having an enjoyable life?

Amy: Well, they say this is Hell, this is … the place that we're living in now is Hell.

Ray: Okay.

Amy: Do you believe in reincarnation or no?

Ray: No, I don't think …

Amy: All kind of religions, all kinds of faiths, but one God.

Ray: Okay.

Amy: Many people worship Him in different ways. Okay. It's how you worship Him in your heart. That's what counts.

Ray: So, this God that you say exists, is He good?

Amy: He's very good. Yes!

Ray: Do you think He should punish murderers and rapists?

Amy: In a certain way. I feel everybody needs some type of punishment, okay.

Ray: Hmm that's interesting.

Amy: … people who do wrong. I don't feel that people should take other people's lives as punishments.

Ray: Let's say somebody's a mass murderer. He gets away with killing, you know, ten women—slitting their throats after he raped them. He's never brought to justice. This happens quite regularly.

Amy: That's right.

Ray: Unsolved crimes. So, what do you think God should do with those people after they die? Do you think He should punish them or just let them go to Heaven?

Amy: I feel that they definitely need punishment. But they don't have to die. They could be punished.

Ray: Let's say they don't feel guilty about it, and they have a really happy life right until the moment they die.

Amy: Oh, no, they ain't going to feel happy. They ain't going to have a happy life.

Ray: So, that's their punishment? They're just not happy?

Amy: They put them in solitary …

Ray: Yeah, but they're not caught, these folks. These people live happy lives right until they die. Okay, let's go back to the … I appreciate you coming on the radio, Amy … Let's go back to Heaven for a moment. Do you think you will go to Heaven?

Amy: Yes.

Ray: You consider yourself to be a good person?

Amy: Yes, I am a good person.

Ray: Okay. Can I ask you a few questions to see if that's true?

Amy: Go ahead.

Ray: Here they are. Number one— Have you ever told a lie?

Amy: Yes. Lot of times.

Ray: Okay, what does that make you? What're you called if you tell a lie?

Amy: Let me tell you something. Let me ask you something.

Ray: Sure.

Amy: Do you … Are you a Christian?

Ray: Yes, ma'am.

Amy: All right, do you eat pork?

Ray: No.

Amy: You okay, well that's good. Have you committed adultery?

Ray: … In my heart, yes.

Amy: Okay, that's not good.

Ray: No, it's bad.

Amy: You can be a Christian who's a hypocrite, right?

Ray: No.

Amy: Some Christians are so strong, so tough that they don't follow the rules.

Ray: That's right.

Amy: They bend the rules.

Ray: Okay, now, ma'am, I have eaten bacon.

Amy: Okay.

Ray: I've made a pig of myself.

Amy: Okay, well what about adultery? What about abortion?

Ray: No, I haven't had an abortion.

Amy: How about, have you lied?

Ray: Yes, ma'am. Hang on. Now, let's go back to ...

Amy: We're all human. Listen, we're all human. God made us all human. We're all vulnerable.

Ray: Yeah.

Amy: ... we all have faults.

Ray: We all eat pork.

Amy: We all make mistakes.

Ray: Yes.

Amy: ... but, God's Son died for us ...

Ray: Before we get there, let's just go back to these four questions because they're important.

Amy: Okay.

Ray: And, I appreciate you sharing that information with me. So, you have told a lie and what're you ... you're called a liar if you lie. Second question—Have you ever stolen something?

Amy: Well, I've never stolen anything.

Ray: And you're not lying to me?

Amy: No, I'm not lying to you.

Ray: Okay. So that's good. Have you ever used God's name in vain?

Amy: I use God's name all the time.

Ray: Do you use it in vain?

Amy: Through prayer.

Ray: Have you ever used His name in vain?

Amy: No.

Ray: Never once?

Amy: I didn't hear you.

Ray: Never once used God's name in vain?

Amy: No.

Ray: Okay. Fourth question—Jesus said if you look with lust, you commit adultery in your heart. Have you ever looked with lust at another person?

Amy: Listen. A lot of the Christians do a lot more than just look with lust.

Ray: Oh, we know that.

Amy: They commit it, okay.

Ray: There are a lot of pretenders around. Yeah, we know that. But have …

Amy: That's right.

Ray: Have you ever looked at someone with lust?

Amy: No. I've been married for thirty-six years.

Ray: Yeah, but before you were married?

Amy: No.

Ray: Well, that's good. You've had pure eyes all your life. Well, there's very bad news, which is sad.

Amy: What?

Ray: The Bible says that all liars will have their place in the Lake of Fire. Jesus said there is a Hell. It's a place of eternal punishment, and God is a God of justice and righteousness, and He set aside a day in which He'll judge the world in righteousness, and God doesn't want you to end up in Hell. Amy, we all have a multitude of sins. I have, every other human being has …

Amy: Everybody.

Ray: That's right.

Amy: Everybody has …

Ray: But we have to give an account of ourselves on the Day of Judgment, not other people …

Amy: Right.

Ray: God's going to punish hypocrites. But, you're going to have to stand before God, and God is going to make manifest every secret sin you've ever committed on the Day of Judgment.

Amy: Definitely.

Ray: And the Scriptures say that if that happens, we'll end up in Hell. The very best of us hasn't kept those Commandments. We've all failed miserably. We have a multitude of sins, and there's nothing we can do about it outside God's grace.

Amy: Mmm.

Ray: So, does it concern you that if you died today, Amy, you'd end up in Hell forever?

Amy: You know what? Let me tell you something. If I died today … it wouldn't be right because I'm not ready. There are a lot of things I have to see, okay. Not for myself. I have a grandson that just came down with leukemia. Ten years old. Now, I'm sure he did not commit major sins. He's ten years old. He just came down with leukemia. Nine years ago, my granddaughter, a year and a half old, caught a virus and it settled in her heart. She had to have a heart transplant.

Ray: Wow.

Amy: Now we turned to God. We turned to God, I told you, daily. I wake up with God's name and I go to bed with God's name, all right.

Ray: Amy …

Amy: So, I believe there's a God.

Ray: Amy …

Amy: He showed me His power.

Ray: Amy, what's your grandson's name? We'll uphold him in prayer

Amy: Smitty.

Ray: What is it?

Amy: Smitty. Actually, if you go to the Web site, it's prayers4smitty.com.

Ray: Okay … Well, our listeners will definitely pray for Smitty.

Amy: Thank you.

Ray: Let's just go back to the question I asked you. Does it concern you that if you died today and God gave you justice, you'd end up in Hell according to the Bible? Does that concern you?

Amy: If that's God's will, I'll take it.

Ray: But it's not God's will. He doesn't want you to perish! He's made a way for you to be completely forgiven.

Amy: Okay.

Ray: All you need is an open and honest heart. Would you like for me to share with you what God did for you so that you wouldn't have to go to Hell?

Amy: Go ahead.

Ray: God became a person in Jesus Christ—a perfect man. Jesus of Nazareth, and then Jesus gave His life on the Cross of Calvary, taking the punishment for the sins that you had committed, that I had committed. The sin of the world was laid upon Him. The Bible says, "He was bruised for our iniquities." When He was on the Cross, this was God Himself paying the fine for that moral law that you and I had broken: His Law, the Ten Commandments, paid in the life's blood of His Son. And then, He rose from the dead and defeated death. And now God, because of what Jesus did on the Cross, can forgive you and dismiss your case. He can commute your death sentence and grant you everlasting life. But what you must do, Amy, is turn from all sin, everything that's abhorrent to God. That is lying and stealing and lusting and blasphemy and even what you're doing—psychic reading that the Bible tells us is an abomination to the Lord, because what you're doing is opening yourself up to familiar spirits.

The moment you turn from sin and trust in Jesus Christ, God says He'll give you a new heart with new desires. You'll know the truth. The truth will make you free. You'll come out of darkness into light. Out of death into life. And God says He'll give you the gift of eternal life. So please think seriously about what we've talked about. Amy, I know none of us thinks that we'll die in the next twenty-four hours, but many of us will. One hundred fifty thousand people …

Amy: That's right.

Ray: ... die every twenty-four hours.

Amy: That's right. Definitely.

Ray: So, please consider these thoughts we've spoken about. Now, do you have any questions?

Amy: All I want is for God to help my grandson. That's the main thing in my life.

Ray: Well, the best thing you can do is get right with God, turn from sin, and you'll have access right into the very throne-room of God, and your prayers will be answered.

Amy: As I told you, He's done it before and He will do it again. I believe in Him one hundred and ten percent.

Ray: But He wants you to be ...

Amy: But we all have our faults. We all have our faults.

Ray: Amy.

Amy: Yes.

Ray: Amy, it's very important to understand that God doesn't want your "belief." All of us believe in God. Every one of us knows that God exists. God wants your obedience.

Amy: Mmm.

Ray: It's by your obedience that you're made right with God. And the only way you can be made right with God is by trusting in Jesus Christ and His shed blood. Thank you so much for listening. We'll remember to pray for Smitty.

Amy: Mmm. God bless you.

Ray: Thank you.

Amy: Bye-bye.

Ray: Bye-bye.

Ray: Ugh. Ugh.

Todd: Well, then. That was interesting, Ray?

Ray: Mmm.

Todd: Aaaaaahhh ...

Ray: You know where my confidence is, Todd?

Todd: Aaaaaaahhhhhhh ...

Ray: The gospel is the power of God unto salvation. It's God that watches over His Word; it's God that's faithful, so we need to pray for Amy and for Smitty, and pray that God brings conviction of sin upon that woman, because she's self-righteous. She's got a multitude of sins. She's probably—more than likely—demon-possessed through generational demonic spirits, so we just pray that God releases her and saves her.

Todd: If you just thought that sounded weird, where else do you think that information comes from, that tells her information like people's names, their circumstances, what's going on? Now they're limited in their knowledge. They certainly don't know the future. That is held only by God Himself, but that is where that information comes from—from demons. There's a wonderful book. It's called *Running Against the Wind* by Bryan Flynn. His life's story of becoming a medium, a psychic, and just flat out confessing they were demons. He had demons inhabiting him that would tell him the information of these people. Zoinks! Now Ray, if that's true, may I ask why didn't you ... she seemed at the end, it's like, "Yeah, listen, thanks very much, but really Smitty, and my son, my grandson is sick." Is there a reason that you maybe didn't come down a little bit harder on her?

Ray: Well, my whole confidence is this—that Legion was filled with demons. Those demons didn't stop him from coming to the foot of the Savior ... the feet of the Savior. He fell at Jesus' feet and cried out, "Have mercy upon me, Lord" so demons can't hinder someone from coming to Christ, and that's my aim. Um ... the way ... the way for her to become rid of those demons is through repentance.

Todd: Oh, yeah.

Ray: In the Name of the Lord.

Todd: I agree completely in that methodology, but she seemed at the end, it's sort of like "Well, you know, that's very nice." And it seems like you could've gone tougher with her to shake … she almost seemed, well, hardly even awakened, let alone alarmed.

Ray: I know. Well, what more can you say but …

Todd: HEY! HEY!

Ray: Amy, open your eyes to the Lake of Fire.

Todd: You're not getting it here. If you died right now, and you've not repented and put your trust in the Savior, you're going to perish.

10

Witnessing to the Antichrist

by Ray Comfort

It promised to be an exciting three days. Kirk was going to meet us in Houston for a seminar. He was flying in from Toronto, Canada, where he was working on the set of *Left Behind III*. EZ, our General Manager, Kirk's mom (Barbara), and I were flying into Dallas from Los Angeles, then onto Houston.

As I walked down the aisle of the plane I greeted one man and offered him a Million Dollar Bill tract. He loved it and made jokes about looking forward to getting the change. This got the attention of the man behind him, so I offered him one also, speaking loud enough for the people behind him to hear what we were talking about. Another dozen or so people wanted them.

When I got to my seat, I passed one to a big man who was sitting behind me. I found out later that this loud-talker's name was Scott. He loved the tract, and kept saying, "This is great." I then passed back a "Department of Annoyance" tract. He loved that even more, and kept raving to EZ (who was now sitting next to him) about how cool it was. Barbara and I smiled at his reaction. Then he blasphemed twice as he talked with EZ. I whispered, "That will come out later as evidence against him." We could hear every word Scott said, whether we wanted to or not.

EZ asked him about himself, and then told him about our TV program, saying that it was a Christian program. (He told us later that the main reason he brought up the things of God at that point was to try and stop Scott from blaspheming.)

EZ asked him, "Have you had a Christian background?"

Scott said he was a Presbyterian, and he began talking about how God had once touched his life. He had cancer and received treatment. One night he was in the hospital and was so sick, he prayed, "God, I think you are punishing me for my sins. Please take me. I can't stand this sickness any longer." He then fell asleep.

The next morning he was better and attributed this healing to God. I thought how it was going to be a little difficult for EZ to now witness to him because Scott believed that there had been divine intervention when he was so sick. How could God be angry with him when He was so gracious to help him in his time of need?

I began praying for God to give EZ wisdom. He gave his own testimony of what God had done in his life. This is the best route to take the conversation because this was EZ's own experience, and couldn't be argued with. He spoke of how he was confronted with God's standard, and then he went through the Commandments, quoting them one by one. He spoke of the reality of Judgment Day and his own guilt before God, of the Cross, repentance, and faith. When EZ reminded Scott about how he had blasphemed twice, he tried to justify himself by saying that he didn't mean anything personal by it. EZ told him that godly Jews won't even speak God's name because they hold it in such reverence, and how they write His name without the vowels, because it is so Holy.

It would have been easy for EZ to now speak of other things. After all, he had gone through the Law and shared the gospel.

He had even confronted Scott about his blasphemy. But he didn't let go. He swung back to the subject of his salvation. He said that the Bible warns that many will try and claim Jesus as Lord, and instead hear the fearful words, "Depart from me, you workers of iniquity. I never knew you." He said that out of the abundance of the heart the mouth speaks. We continued to listen to the conversation:

"I hope I'm not offending you."

"No. No you're not."

"There's nothing more important than your salvation. Are you truly a Christian? Are you born again? I heard you talking to your mother on the phone. It's obvious that you love her. How would you feel if a man broke into her home, beat, and raped her? Do you think that such a person should be brought to justice?"

"Of course."

EZ then talked with him about the reasonableness of judgment.

Scott asked why God didn't intervene in court cases when someone was obviously guilty of some terrible crime. Why was He unable to touch the jury? It was an interesting question.

"God can intervene, but He lets many things run their courses," EZ said. Scott said that he couldn't accept the Genesis account of creation. He was a mathematician. He saw things as black and white. There was a huge amount of scientific evidence to back up evolution as opposed to creation. EZ didn't argue with him. He didn't let evolution become a big issue.

There are many questions people have about life's origins and why God allows and doesn't allow certain things to happen. They may be legitimate questions, but they shouldn't stop us from getting right with Him. If you are sinking into quicksand and there's only one hand offering to pull you out, you may have legitimate questions about the person offering the help. Why does he wear a gold ring? Why does he have a scar on his hand? But they are not of immediate importance. Let him pull you out of your danger; then ask the questions. But the odds are that they then won't seem too important.

EZ said that he would like to send Scott *The Evidence Bible*, saying that it would help to answer his questions. Fortunately, two hours earlier I had slipped one into my bag. I found it and handed it to EZ. Scott was delighted, leaned over, and shook my hand. We then asked if it was okay to mail him a copy of our evolution episode of "The Way of the Master." He said that he would love to receive it, and added, "Actually, it was quite fortuitous that I should run into you." He looked at the Bible and said, "I'm touched that you gave me this." Then he said, "This has been an absolute delight." He was right.

Fruit and Nut Section

We had planned to do a seminar in Houston and then take a team and preach open-air. About 600 people showed up for the seminar and another 200 had registered for the open-air. As we made our way out the door, it began to rain. Fortunately, our host, Brannon Howse, had made provision for rain. He had permission from the owners of a supermarket to conduct the open-air in the fruit and nut section of their store.

To our delight, that's what happened. I stood up in the huge modern supermarket on a plastic milk crate and preached the gospel to the large crowd that gathered. Then Kirk also stood up and preached. It was an amazing and fruitful experience.

We conducted another seminar in Dallas, each preached in a large church, and then flew to Canada.

As we stood in the Toronto airport, a man with Middle Eastern features asked if we wanted a taxi. As we walked toward his vehicle, I caught up with him, asked his name, and inquired how long he had been driving. Mike had been a taxi driver for six years—something he enjoyed much more than his previous job. As he put our luggage into the trunk, Kirk smiled and whispered to me,

"The pit bull is already into action. The teeth are already in ..."

He also likens me to a humming bird. I like both analogies. Christians should always be moving quickly with the precision of a finely tuned machine, but at the same time be as stubborn as pit bulls—we should be "steadfast, unmovable, always abounding in the work of the Lord" (1 Corinthians 15:58). Humming bulls.

Mike was an Egyptian man who had been living in Canada since the age of ten years. I told him that we were there for a Christian movie called *Left Behind.*

"Have you had a Christian background?"

"Catholic."

Was he a good person? He thought so. So we went through the Ten Commandments. Twice he said, "This has been a rude awakening."

Then he said, "This is making me feel sorry for my sins."

I asked EZ and Kirk if they wanted to say anything. They did. EZ talked about the fact that he visited New York just after 9/11, and how in a moment of time, 3,000 people were swept into eternity. He talked to Mike about the danger of having a hardened heart toward God and gave an analogy about how wolves are caught in Alaska. Blood-soaked meat, laced with sharp razors, is left in the snow. The wolves are attracted by the smell of blood and begin to lick the frozen meat. The ice numbs their tongues as they lick, and because of the numbness, they fail to feel the pain as the blades cut into their tongues. This creates more blood, which they don't realize is their own, so they keep licking the sharp blades, and eventually bleed to death.

EZ told Mike that sin had a pleasurable but numbing effect on the human heart, and because sin numbed, it would eventually take his life. Kirk added his own experience of once being an atheist, and about the importance of reading the Bible.

I asked Mike where he would go if he died at that moment.

"Hell."

"When are you going to get right with God?"

"As soon as possible."

"What about tonight? If you like, we can pray with you when we arrive at our destination."

"I would like to do that."

Mike pulled his van over at our destination, and we had thirty seconds' silence as he got his heart right with God. Then I prayed for him. He thanked us a number of times, adding once again, "This has been a wake up call." We gave him some CDs and a book, and he hugged us as we parted.

The next morning we were on the set of *Left Behind*. Kirk asked if I was going to try and witness to Brad Johnson. Brad was the actor who played Reyford Steel. He was a tall, handsome man, and was once voted one of the top fifty best looking men on the planet. Kirk and his wife Chelsea had spoken to him about the things of God, but although Brad's wife was a Christian, he leaned towards atheism. I told Kirk that I was excited to talk to him about his beliefs.

When I saw him standing alone, I walked up to him and said, "Hey Brad, tell me about your beliefs. I hear you're an atheist."

"I'd rather not get into a discussion while I'm working."

"But I would love to speak with you. I'm fascinated by atheism."

"I would like to have a debate with you. How about we talk when I'm not working?"

"I will hold you to that."

He then reached out his hand to shake on it.

As we shook hands, I told him that I had written a book called *God Doesn't Believe in Atheists*, and that I was invited be a platform speaker at American Atheists, Inc. I added that I love talking with atheists because I can prove God's existence in two minutes.

"I'm not really an atheist. Religion is a personal thing."

"I agree with you. The world would be better without it *(religion)*. What offends most people are hypocrites. But the key is to understand the meaning of the word 'hypocrite.' It means 'pretender.' They are not the real thing, and God will sort out the genuine from the false on the Day of Judgment."

Later that day I saw him standing alone once again, so I told him that I was leaving the next morning and would love to get with him before then.

"Okay, then. Tell me this. Do you believe in Noah and the ark?"

"Of course."

"How could predators be in the same boat with animals they devour? Barring divine intervention, there's no way it could work."

"But that's why it worked. There *was* divine intervention. I not only believe in Noah; I believe in Jonah, Samson, Adam, and Eve, and all the 'silly' stories, and there is a good reason that I believe."

Just then a makeup lady asked him to sit in a chair that was set up a short distance from where we stood.

"Come over with me and we will continue this." I was delighted.

As he sat in the chair, he listened intently as I told him about how I once ran a kid's club. I asked one hundred of them to line up for candy. As I studied the line, I realized that I had a line of greed in front of me, so I went to the other end and took great delight in giving the candy out to the weak and sickly kids first.

Brad continued to listen as I told him that in this world, where the rich get richer and the poor get stomped on, God goes to the other end of the line. The Bible says that the poor heard Jesus gladly.

"The way God turned the line around was by using 'foolish things to confound the wise' (1 Corinthians 1:27). Anyone who has pride and intellectual dignity would never stoop to believe such foolish stories. Behold the wisdom of God. The door to enter into Heaven is very low."

Brad added, "So that only the humble may enter. You are very passionate about this."

"It's more than passionate. You're like a blind man heading for a thousand foot cliff. I desperately want you to turn around."

"I don't agree with using fear like that."

I said, "Do you remember a TV advertisement years ago that had some dummies in a car as it went into a head-on collision? A deep voice asked, 'What goes through the head of a dummy in a head-on collision if he's not wearing a seat belt? The steering wheel. Don't be a dummy. Buckle up!' That's the use of fear. But it's legitimate. It *is* fearful to be in a head-on collision and not be wearing a seat belt, and it's a fearful thing to be in your sins on Judgment Day."

"My kids are always talking to me like this." The implication was that neither they nor I would do much good, because he had his mind made up.

As we parted I said, "Do you love your beliefs more than you love your kids?" I couldn't help but feel that God had something to do with that question because I could feel that it irritated him.

He replied, "I don't need to answer that ..." We parted, but I was pleased to see that he came across and chatted with Kirk and me about half an hour later.

The Antichrist
Kirk joined EZ and me for lunch. As we spoke, he said, "There's the Antichrist." Sure enough, two tables over we saw Gordon

Currie, the actor who played the Antichrist in the previous two movies. He looked a little different with glasses as he chatted with people at their table. He saw Kirk and walked over to our table.

Gordon had a very warm personality and a wonderful, loud laugh. They chatted for about ten minutes; we all shook hands and he walked away. I followed him and said, "Gordon. I have a gift for you." As he turned around I handed him a CD called "What Hollywood Believes."

He looked at the celebrity names on the cover and said, "Brad Pitt. I shared an apartment with him."

"That's interesting. Have you had a Christian background?"

"I'm spiritual, but not religious."

"What do you think happens after someone dies?"

"I don't necessarily believe in Heaven and Hell. I believe in karma."

"If there is a Heaven, do you think you would make it? Do you consider yourself to be a good person?"

Then I went through the Commandments. He had violated most of them, and I added that karma is a form of idolatry. It dismisses the fact that God warns that He will judge the world in righteousness and reduces the concept of His character to that of something He's not.

He was very congenial as he asked me about other religions. "Are they all wrong?"

"They come from the concept that man thinks that he can bribe God to forgive his sins, and to therefore let him live. This is because they don't realize that God's standards are infinitely above ours. Christianity is not a Western religion; it originated in the East."

We spoke for about twenty minutes, after which I inquired if he had a Bible.

"Brad Pitt gave me one," he said.

We then shook hands and parted. In the light of what I learned about Brad Pitt's spirituality, I was amazed that he gave him a Bible.

Things Don't Always Go Well

It was very early in the morning. EZ walked on the deep Toronto snow in a way that betrayed that he was from California. He walked like a cat walks on a wet surface. The driver opened the taxi door and we jumped into our airport transportation.

"Hi. What's your name?"

"Tom."

"Tom, thanks for getting up so early to take us to the airport."

"No problem. I do it all the time."

A little small talk, then I asked, "So, have you seen the *Left Behind* movies?"

"No."

"Have you had a Christian background?"

"No."

"What do you think happens after you die ... do you think about it?"

"Yes, I do."

"Do you believe in Heaven and Hell?"

"Yes."

"Where do you think you will go?"

"That's a silly question."

"So you think that you will go to Heaven?"

"Of course."

"You're a good person?"

"Absolutely."

We went through the Good Test. "Tom, by your own admission, you are a lying, blasphemous adulterer at heart. If

God judges you by the Ten Commandments, do you think that you will be innocent or guilty?"

"I don't think God is like that. I think that He is forgiving."

"Tom, do you know what that's called? It's called 'idolatry.' It's when you make a god to suit yourself—a god you feel comfortable with. It's actually a transgression of the Second of the Ten Commandments."

Tom's attitude changed. His voice firmed as he said, "I need to concentrate on my driving, so let's not talk any longer. I don't want to smash this van."

"Don't worry. I will pay for it if you crash. This is too important not to talk. If you crash and we get killed, EZ and I will go to Heaven, but you will go to Hell."

He became angry and said, "Let's not talk about this any longer. I don't want you telling me that I will go to Hell."

"I'm sorry for offending you. That wasn't my intention."

Dead cold silence. The three of us sat in the van and looked at the road in front of us for a long two minutes.

I asked, "Do you have a family?"

"Yes. Three boys. Teenagers."

"Do you go fishing?"

He did. In fact he became quite chatty about fishing despite having to concentrate on his driving.

As we approached the airport, I said, "Tom, again, I'm sorry for offending you. Here's $20 for your help and a gift."

"You don't need to do this."

"I would like to. And here's a CD with celebrities' beliefs."

He smiled warmly, took it, and wished us a friendly farewell.

11

Witnessing to
Jehovah's Witnesses

by Ray Comfort

The question arises: do these principles work with the cults? To answer that, let me share an experience I had some time ago.

I rushed down the stairs to the sound of a barking dog and our doorbell. When I opened it, two well-dressed young men stood in front of me. I greeted them with a warm, "Hi," to which one of them asked in perfect English, "Do you know of any Spanish speaking families around here?"

"Next door there is a Spanish speaking family. Across the road there is an Indonesian family, then an Indian, then English, and I am Chinese. Do you want to see a picture of me on a cruise?"

They politely said they did, so I quickly opened my wallet and showed them a picture of Tom Cruise with the word "ME" on his forehead. They laughed. I then did some sleight of hand, where I turn two one-dollar bills into a five. They were impressed.

"So, what are you guys selling?"

"Nothing."

"Are you Mormons?"

"No."

"Jehovah's Witnesses?"

"Yes."

"Tell me this. I have a knife in my back. I have three minutes to live. My blood and life are draining from me. I know I'm dying. What are you going to say to me? How can I enter the Kingdom?"

They looked at each other, then back at me. There was dead silence. It was obvious that they didn't know what to tell me.

"Come on, guys. I'm dying. I have three minutes!"

One of them said, "I don't know. There's a lot you have to do."

The other one echoed, "Lots!"

Then the first said, "You have to learn. You have to gain knowledge ..."

"What about the thief on the cross? What knowledge did he get? How could he learn anything? He couldn't turn the pages of a book—he was nailed to a cross. He probably couldn't read anyway. Yet Jesus said to him, 'Today you will be with Me in Paradise.'"

"We have to go now."

"Come on, guys. This is important. I want to know how to enter Jehovah's Kingdom. What are your names?"

"Jonathan."

"Javier."

"Do you consider yourself to be good people?"

"Um ... yes."

"Have you ever told a lie?"

"Yes."

"What does that make you?"

"A liar."

Javier said he had stolen and then became very quiet. Jonathan said that he had never stolen, blasphemed, or even looked at a woman with lust. Never.

"Are you gay?"

"No. The reason I haven't done that is because I was born into the truth."

I explained, "We have to face a perfect Law on the Day of Judgment and nothing you and I do can save us. Only the blood of Jesus. He died for us. He took our punishment upon Himself, and now God can save us through His mercy. That's why the thief was saved. He didn't do anything to save himself because he couldn't. Only God's mercy and grace can save us. The Bible says, 'For by grace are you saved through faith, and that not of yourselves. It is the gift of God, not of works lest any man boast' (Ephesians 2: 8-9). 'Not by works of righteousness that we have done has He saved us, but according to His mercy' (Titus 3:5). Revelation 21:8 says that all liars will have their part in the Lake of Fire. That why you need Jesus Christ—to wash your sins away. The moment you repent and trust Him, God will forgive you and grant you everlasting life."

"But we are doing what Jesus did."

"Did He go door to door?"

"Yes. He went around preaching the gospel."

"But the gospel you are preaching is different than the one He preached. The Bible says that there's nothing you and I can do to merit Jehovah's favor—to earn everlasting life. We are saved by God's mercy. That's how the thief on the cross could be saved. We are not saved by doing anything."

"Does that mean I can believe in Jesus and then run around lying and stealing?"

"No. That's hypocrisy, and no hypocrite will enter the Kingdom. You have to repent and trust Jesus Christ alone for your salvation, and not try and bribe Jehovah. I don't do good works and preach the gospel to be forgiven. I do it because I *am* forgiven, and the difference is life and death, Heaven and Hell. Thanks, guys, for talking to me."

"Thank you."

There were no arguments about the deity of Christ because I made sure the conversation didn't go in that direction. It's important to remember that Jehovah's Witnesses see Christians as misguided 'Trinitarians,' while they jealously guard Jehovah's glory. So they are going to be incredibly stubborn about the issue of Jehovah's sharing His glory with another.

Do you remember who revealed the truth about the deity of Jesus to Peter? When he said that Jesus was the Christ, the Son of the Living God, Jesus said to him, "Blessed are you, Simon Bar-Jonah, for flesh and blood has not revealed this to you, but My Father who is in Heaven." So I believe that the best way for anyone to find out who Jesus is, is for God to reveal it to them. If I had started quoting Bible verses to make some point about Jesus being God, they would have started quoting back, and then they would have fallen back on the argument that they have the only true translation. Jehovah's Witnesses also deny the existence of Heaven and Hell. They believe in annihilation and that the Kingdom of God will come to this earth and be set up for a thousand years. Christians can't even agree on issues of prophecy, so I deliberately stayed away from it.

All I did was hold up the truth against error and left the results in the hands of God. Charles Spurgeon said, "I have heard it said that if there is a crooked stick, and you want to show how crooked it is, you need not waste words in description. Place a straight one by the side of it, and the thing is done directly."

All religions have their roots in idolatry. They have a wrong understanding of the nature of God and His righteous requirements. When you look closely at their beliefs, it becomes evident they are made up of the fruitless branches of self-righteousness. They think that they can bribe God with their works. Like the Jews of whom Paul spoke—they go about to establish their own righteousness, being ignorant of the righteousness which is of God (see Romans 10:3). The Law puts the axe to the root. It reveals a perfect righteousness and kills hope of self-salvation. It shows the self-righteous person that the leap he is trying to make to Heaven is infinitely beyond his reach.

I had noticed that Javier had been nodding in agreement at what I was saying. When he asked for my name again, I looked directly at him and said that they could come back any time. We shook hands and parted on good terms. I came away feeling really good because I had avoided doing what the Bible says not to do—to argue:

"But avoid foolish and ignorant disputes, knowing that they generate strife. And a servant of the Lord must not quarrel but be gentle to all, able to teach, patient, in humility correcting those who are in opposition, if God perhaps will grant them repentance, so that they may know the truth, and that they may come to their senses and escape the snare of the devil, having been taken captive by him to do his will" (2 Timothy 2:23-26).

12

Left Behind III: The Disco Version

by Kirk Cameron

I am writing this on the airplane flying home from Toronto, Canada, after three weeks of filming this supernatural thriller movie, *Left Behind III*. It was incredible.

Once again, I'm playing "Buck," and my wife, Chelsea, plays "Hattie." This time, the Trib Force is doing all they can to slow down the plans of Nicholae Carpathia to annihilate Christians from the planet (by secretly infecting the majority of Bibles with a highly toxic biological agent like anthrax and allowing the Trib Force to distribute them to new converts), and bring in his new, one-world government and religion. This movie has the famous double wedding scene between Buck and Chloe and Rayford and Amanda. Hattie is pregnant with the antichrist's child and Bruce Barns goes home to be with the Lord.

While there are many BIG scenes (exploding limousines, the White House engulfed in flames, demonic deception, special effects, etc.), my favorite scene is when Buck witnesses to the president of the United Sates. Well-known actor Lou Gossett, Jr. plays "President Fitzhugh" and he does an incredible job. While we were filming this scene, the air was thick with smoke, flames burned outside the windows of the Oval Office, and I was able to share the gospel biblically (sin, righteousness, judgment to come, grace, repentance, and faith) on camera. Lou so threw himself into the role that he began to weep as he prayed to receive the Lord and ask for forgiveness. To think that SONY will be distributing this movie (with clear gospel content) in Wal-Mart is mind-boggling.

During one scene Buck bursts into the president's office and stands in the doorway, silhouetted by the flames and surrounded by white smoke. I thought it would be funny to "strike a pose" and have the photographer grab the shot. Well, he did, and it turned into a huge advertising campaign for the movie! "Behind Buck is a Disco-Duck!"

While I (and Ray Comfort and other friends) had many opportunities to share the gospel with unsaved cast and crew members, including Gordon Currie (Nicholae) and Brad Johnson (Rayford Steele), as well as the makeup artist and several transportation drivers, I knew that I still hadn't witnessed to the director and most of the crew (except for conducting myself professionally on the set). I had one last opportunity to do something for eternity. I knew what I wanted to do. I had been thinking about it for two days. I was rehearsing it in my mind over and over. I was *very* nervous.

On my final day, after shooting my last scene, we broke for lunch. Most of the crew, the producers, and some cast (about 50 people) were in one room eating their food. I prayed that God would help me "open my mouth boldly as I ought to speak." I swallowed the rhinoceros-sized ball of fear in my throat, stood in the middle of the room, and said, "Excuse me, everyone. Could I have your attention for a moment?" Everyone stopped eating and looked up at me. I just about passed out. My ears turned red and my mouth went dry, but I couldn't turn back. I can perform or preach in front of thousands, but when it comes to opening my mouth for the gospel, it all flies out the window.

I could hear a pin drop. I thanked them all for being so kind to my wife and me during the filming, and for working so hard in the cold without complaining (sometimes until 6:30 a.m., outside, in subzero temperatures). Then I said, "People often ask me on the streets about the spiritual conversations that must have taken place on the set of a movie like *Left Behind*—after all, it's all about God and faith in Jesus Christ. Well, the truth is, I haven't heard many people talking about spiritual things on this set, so I'd like to share something very personal with you." By this time, I think I had everyone's attention—the Jewish photographer, the French-Canadian atheists, the new-age hair dressers, the Catholic makeup artist, some foul mouthed production crew members, and even a couple of the producers. I told them about my background as an atheist and how I was captured by the love of Christ fourteen years ago. I told them, "This may be the last time I get to talk with you, so I'd appreciate it if you would consider what I'm about to say."

I told them that many people grow up with religion and have seen the Cross, but have never seen the love of God in the Cross. "They don't see the love of God because they don't see their sin. They don't see their sin because they have never looked into the mirror of God's Commandments to see themselves clearly. So let's have a look." I spoke about sin, God's righteous standards by which He will judge them on Judgment Day, the penalty of Hell, and then about Grace, the Cross, the sacrifice of the Son of God, and the need for "repentance toward God and faith towards the Lord Jesus Christ." I then told them that I realized that I had made myself a fool in the eyes of some, but that I didn't have a choice because I so cared about them and where they spend eternity. I thanked them for listening and sat down at an empty table to eat my lunch.

There I sat for five long minutes. No applause. No "thank you's" or "Atta boy's." Just people going back to their dinners and conversations. One producer later commented, "It takes a lot of [testosterone] to do what you did," and the Jewish photographer said, "While I don't agree with you, that took a lot of courage. Kudos to you."

I slept sweetly that night. My confidence was in the power of the gospel and in God's faithfulness to watch over those who would come to believe in the Lord Jesus. Only Heaven knows exactly what happened in the spiritual realm that evening. I'm glad it's over, and I'm on my way back to see my family.

There's a man sitting next to me right now on the airplane that doesn't believe there is a God. His name is Graham, and he's from New Zealand. I'm going to try my best to help him see the truth before we land. Maybe I'll break the ice by asking him if he's interested in seeing a poster for the new movie called *Left Behind III: the Disco Version*.

Incidentally, I later received this email from one of the *Left Behind* movie producers:

> Hey, Kirk,
>
> It was great working with you once again, and I know you'll be pleased with the finished film. Your talk at lunchtime to the crew the other day certainly stirred many people up. I had more people to talk to and answer questions about faith and sin and Jesus Christ than ever before.
>
> Two crew members came to me and said they thought your talk was great and that they were amazed at how upset some people were that you did that. They noted that if you had told an awful story or dirty joke nobody would have said anything. But since you shared something wholesome and uplifting, you made many angry.
>
> Thanks for sharing, Kirk ... many have been affected. Oh, and Krysta, (part of the EPK team) was

especially touched and will be heading to church this weekend with Sue Rogers. The Spirit is definitely working on her.

Thought you'd want to know.

God Bless, André

13

Never. Ever.

by Ray Comfort

B ack in the early 1980s it was a standing joke in our church
that I would never go to India. Never. Ever. There were a
number of reasons. The endless travel. Garlic. The unbearable
heat. Bloodsucking mosquitoes. Malaria. India was not a place
for Comfort.

It was November 2004. EZ, my son-in-law, had arranged
for me to speak to the staff of Gospel for Asia in Dallas, Texas,
and he said that the president of the huge and respected
missionary organization, KP Yohannon, had asked to see me.
As we were driving there, I told EZ not to let KP talk me into
going to India. I wouldn't go there.

An hour or so later we drove away from the building with
a sense of excitement that I would be going to India to speak. I
had no idea what had happened. I could hardly believe that I
had changed my mind. During our meeting, the persuasive
preacher had told me to cancel every other speaking
engagement, because what I would say to the prospective
pastors at his Bible school could change the nation.

A few days later I was back in California. I called EZ and
said that I didn't want to go. I had changed my mind. That
night I awoke and heard the words, "His word is his bond,"

echo in my mind. During the next day, I remembered where I had heard those words. They were from a book that I had just written in which I stressed the absolute importance of a godly man keeping his word. If he said that he would do something, he would do it even if it caused him great distress. I called EZ and told him that I would go there to keep my word despite the travel, the mosquitoes, etc.

Three months later, EZ and I were sitting in business class of a plane as we flew to Germany on our way to India. A Chicago millionaire had heard about our trip, and without even checking with us, bumped us up to the business class for the round trip. God bless him. God made man to walk upright, but he was made to lie down to sleep. Some people can sleep for long spells while seated. I can't. I drift off for about twenty minutes and wake up with a crick in my neck. By the time I reach my destination on a long flight, I'm exhausted. But not so in the business class. Instead of being crammed in with the cattle, we were sitting in La-Z-Boys, indulging in fine dining.

No doubt there was a buzz among Indian mosquitoes that they were in for a delicious treat, but I had made my provision for the flesh. I had purchased a mosquito net, two different repellents, repellent "wipes" (with 30 percent DEET), and garlic pills. Mosquitoes (like most of us) hate the smell of garlic. The little beasts were not going to dine on my blood.

As we landed in Germany on our way to India, both EZ and I felt refreshed after a good sleep. We had prayed that God would order our steps, and ordered they were. International travel was a breeze … that is, until the plane landed a little late and we missed our connecting flight! We missed it by three minutes. Suddenly, life became complicated. Missing that flight meant that we would miss our connecting flight within India. We stopped and thanked God that all things worked together for those who were called according to His purposes (Romans 8:28). For the next two hours we went from counter to counter as German-accented agents booked us on another flight.

As we waited to board, suddenly EZ let out an incredulous, "There's KP!" Sure enough, standing by the counter was KP Yohannon. Amazingly, he was on his way to Bombay from New York to a speaking engagement, and happened to be on the same flight on which we had re-booked. He had missed his mileage to upgrade to business class and was seated about fifteen feet from us on the plane. He made some quick calls on his cell phone to our destination to tell them about the new flights. Then he said that he and a friend would travel with us to make sure we made it to our destination.

As we sat on the flight, I asked the gentleman next to me if he would mind swapping seats with KP. He was very happy to do so. I gave him a copy of *What Hollywood Believes* as a token of appreciation and also a consolation for my conscience in that I couldn't witness to him, but at least he would have a Christian book in his possession.

KP Yohannon is a wonderful man of God. I had read his book and knew that this was a man who had a passion for souls. He was courageous enough to say that missionaries were not called to build hospitals and orphanages. They were commanded to primarily preach Christ crucified. Most modern missionaries had substituted good works for the preaching of the gospel, and KP told them so.

During the flight I questioned him. What was the key to the "success" of his ministry? He said that it was a simple faithfulness to God. What was the biggest hindrance to the gospel in India? It was the modern Church with its modern message. He also had a wonderful grip on the importance of the Law in the gospel presentation. He told me about a teaching he had heard where the preacher spoke of Doctor Law and Doctor Grace. Doctor Law could only prescribe death for the patient, and when he was without hope, the doctor took him by the hand to the door of Doctor Grace, saying that Grace could help him. When the patient invited Doctor Law into the office of Doctor Grace, he said that he couldn't enter.

As the four of us sat in an airport restaurant in Bombay, I did a little sleight of hand for a young man, who then politely listened to me as I struggled to witness to him. He hardly spoke any English, but as I took him through the Law with some charades, this Hindu man was able to understand that Jesus died on the Cross for him. He said, "I have friends ... taking me to church. Jesus is God." I was very encouraged by his last statement and gave him a "What Hollywood Believes" CD and some tracts, for which he was very grateful.

I then began to do some writing on my laptop and noticed that two men at the next table were speaking English. One of them used filthy language so many times, I closed my laptop and decided that I had better witness to him.

I said, "Where are you guys headed? Are you from the States?"

"Montana."

Mr. Foul-mouth didn't answer. I gave them each a Million Dollar Bill tract and a "Department of Annoyance" card. Mr. Montana was amused. Mr. Foul-mouth was not impressed. I decided to sink or swim.

"They are gospel tracts. What do you think happens after someone dies?" Montana clammed up and Foul-mouth said, "I don't care."

I asked if he was an atheist. He was, but seemed a little shaky in his conviction.

"I had two guys come to my door once and talk about this stuff. I really don't care about it."

"Mormons?"

"Yeah."

"I'm not saying the same things as they did."

"Yes, you are. They *(Mormons)* asked if I *(Mr. Foul-mouth)* wanted to see my relatives in Heaven. I told them I didn't want to see my wife. I want to see an eighteen-year-old Korean virgin."

"Do you mind talking about this stuff?"

"Not at all. I don't care about it."

"I'm Ray. What's your name?"

"Andy."

"Andy, would you sell one of your eyes for a million dollars?"

"Of course not."

"So you are then telling me that your eyes are without price, and you don't care about whether you lose your life that looks out though them! Don't you care about your life?"

"I do."

"What if there's such a place as Hell?"

"I don't care."

"Well, let's do a test. This really helped me. Do you consider yourself to be a good person?"

He did, so I took him through the Commandments, and he proved to be a lying, thieving, blasphemous adulterer at heart.

"Do you think that you will be innocent or guilty on the Day of Judgment—if God judges you by the Ten Commandments?"

"I don't believe in God."

"I said, 'If.'"

"Guilty."

"Heaven or Hell?"

"I'd be on my way to Hell. But, listen. Do you believe that people lived until they were 600 years old?"

"Yes. I believe it was up to 965 years old."

He gave a skeptical laugh and asked, "Who do you know of who lived to 965 years old?"

"Methuselah."

It was as though Andy had just proved his case. He said, "There you are. That's from the Bible. Science says otherwise. No one could live until they were that age."

As far as he was concerned, the argument was all over. The Bible is full of stupid stories and I was an idiot to believe it.

"Andy. Think of this. If *National Geographic* published a story saying that scientists had just discover human bones in South America in which tests proved that the person lived for that long, you'd believe it."

He hesitated to answer.

I said, "You have got blind faith in science. Anyway, I want to thank you for listening to me. I really appreciate it."

I asked him if I could give him a gift (I wanted to give him a CD), but he said he wouldn't take anything from me. We then shook hands and parted. I kept Andy in prayer and thanked God that he had listened for as long as he did.

Towards the end our journey, we sat crammed in with the cattle. The man stuffed his bag under the seat in front of him and sat down next to me, holding a book.

"Good book?"

"Yes. I have just started it."

He passed it to me for my perusal. It was by an American author on how to succeed in business. I recognized the publisher and flicked to the back. Sure enough, there was a Christian message. There was no mention of sin or judgment. It was the ever-popular message of "God has a wonderful plan for your life—go for it, do what you want to do and God will bless you because He loves business initiative." I pointed it out and asked if he was a Christian. He wasn't.

I then introduced myself. His name was Prashand. It was a 90-minute flight, so I sat back and minutes later, both of us were sound asleep, sitting up.

When we awoke for breakfast I said, "Tell me about Hinduism. What do Hindus believe happens after death?"

"There is rebirth. Depending on what good deeds you have done. Hinduism doesn't believe in a Heaven and a Hell, as Christianity does."

"Do *you* believe in Heaven and in Hell?"

"Yes."

"Are you a Hindu?"

"Yes."

"Do you think that you will go to Heaven?"

"Yes. I think so."

"Here's something that helped me understand the issue."

I then took him through the Good Test. He had lied and admitted that he was a liar, but said that he hadn't stolen. Nor had he used God's name in vain.

"Prashand, this one nailed me to the wall. It will you, too. Jesus said, 'Whoever looks upon a woman to lust after her has committed adultery already with her in his heart.' Have you ever done that? Even once?"

"Once or twice."

"Listen to this—this is how God sees you. By your own admission, you are a lying adulterer at heart. If God judges you by the Ten Commandments on the Day of Judgment, do you think that you will be innocent or guilty?"

"Guilty."

"Heaven or Hell?"

"I think that I would still go to Heaven."

"Why?"

"Because of my good deeds."

"You can't make it to Heaven. This is why. God sees all your sins. You said that you had lusted 'once or twice.' God knows exactly how many times, and I'm sure it's more than that. Like every red-blooded male, no doubt, it's thousands of times." He didn't disagree.

"Prashand, God sees your thought-life. He has seen every time you have looked at a woman with lust and He has seen all those other sins. He sees you from a standard of perfection."

"But I have done good things."

"Think of it like this. A man rapes a woman and viciously beats her. The judge says, 'You are guilty,' and the criminal answers, 'Yes, judge, but I have done many good deeds.' The judge would say, 'What has that got to do with your crime? You are guilty and you must be punished.'"

Prashand nodded in solemn agreement.

"So you would be guilty and end up in Hell."

He had a sober expression, so I said, "Do you know what God did for you so that you wouldn't have to end up in Hell? He sent His Son Jesus to suffer and die for you. When Jesus was on the Cross He took the punishment for your sins, for my sins and the sins of the whole world. If you repent and trust in Him, God will dismiss your case, because Jesus paid your fine in His life's blood."

Then I told him that he must repent and trust in the Savior.

He said, "Most people believe in Karma."

"I know. But that isn't going to work on Judgment Day. God gave us a conscience. The word means 'with knowledge.' When we lie, steal, lust, murder, blaspheme, commit adultery, etc., we do it with knowledge that it's wrong. Our own reason, civil law, and the Bible make it clear that good works will not wash away sin. It's like handing the judge a bribe."

Prashand was nodding in agreement. I asked him if he had a Bible. He didn't, so I gave him one and a copy of *What Hollywood Believes*. He was very grateful. I thanked him for listening to me and we parted when the flight ended.

I then began the last leg of our journey. So far we had traveled for 32 hours, and we now had a three-hour drive to the Bible school.

Have you ever been on a roller coaster? One of those terrifying speed machines designed to take you to the edge of death itself, and then bring you back? That's what it's like to drive in India. In the United States the yellow line down the middle of a two-way road has a purpose. It is saying, "Right— Life. Left—Death." In India that line means nothing. To drive at an oncoming vehicle at 75 m.p.h. in the United States and swerve away at the very last minute is called "Playing Chicken."

In India it is normal driving. It seemed that the sight of an oncoming bus was a sign for the driver to overtake the car in front of him.

In the United States, if you drove around honking your horn every thirty seconds at almost every other driver, it would speed your trip to Heaven. In India it is a courtesy. "Honk, honk, honk, honk" means "I'm coming through—thank you, sir. Would you be kind enough to move your vehicle over for me?" More honking is your way of saying "Thanks." (A few days later, we were driven to some stores to buy gifts to take home. We drove for about 20 miles and I counted 193 honks of the horn.)

The sights and sounds made busy New York seem dull. Trucks, motorbikes, buses, cars, bikes laden with people. Everywhere there were people, many were standing at the very edge and even on the road, seeming to say to the honking speedster, "Hit me if you can." Mangy dogs, goats, ducks, cows, bulls, rice fields, workers, billboards—thousands of them, people carrying things, sitting sidesaddle on motor bikes, the jungles, brown uniformed police, the colorful clothing—the sights, sounds, and smells that could only be India. I could understand why people either loved or hated this great county. The drive was a culture shock—three hours of incredible, fascinating, memorable, mouth-stopping terror. It was sensory overload.

The Gospel for Asia compound was incredible. Magnificent buildings were scattered over one hundred acres that cut into the jungles of India. Yet, we were told that 90 percent of Gospel for Asia's buildings were in Northern India. The people were very friendly and incredibly respectful. They hung onto every word uttered from the pulpit. The culture was so different from that of the United States. People wobbled their heads from side to side, sometimes as a greeting, sometimes saying that they agreed with you. It was a different culture, but their love for

God was evident in their commitment to the gospel. My hope was that I would be able to leave them with a good impression of this little mustached man with a strange accent. I'm sure I left an impression on at least four Indian students the day before we left to return to the States. I gave a friendly "Hi, guys," as they walked by. Our interpreter smiled slightly and whispered the Indian meaning of the word "guys." He said, "You just called them 'cows'"

What Do You Do?

On the flight back to the U.S. we had a layover in Madras. The flight there was crowded. As EZ and I sat next to each other, I saw a man pick up his briefcase off the floor. Unfortunately the woman in the seat in front of him had the tassel of her colorful garment caught in the clip of the case. She spent a moment trying to release it as he held his case. I smiled at him and he whispered, "It's embarrassing when that happens." I saw the incident as an opportunity to hand him a Department of Annoyance tract. He took it, looked at it, and passed me his business card. His name was Gopakumar and he was involved in "Technology Solutions." He was a native Indian, but he lived in the United States. A few minutes later I heard him laugh as he reread my "card." He leaned across the aisle and said, "What do you do?"

"I write books and co-host a TV show in which we teach Christians how to share their faith. Do you think much about what happens after death?"

"I believe that Heaven and Hell are on this earth."

He then told me that Hinduism, Jesus, Moses, and Mohammad had some good things to say. He spoke about how many million gods there are, and how Hinduism is scientific by nature. He even said that what we believe, even if it's wrong, can be very beneficial for us.

I let him talk for some time, keeping my eye on how long it would be until the flight ended. I only needed a few minutes.

After he had shared his beliefs, I asked him if he would sell his eyes for a million dollars. He wouldn't. I said that he was taking the ultimate gamble by having his own beliefs. What if Moses and Jesus were right about the Day of Judgment? I asked him if he had ever heard the Christian message, and when he said that he hadn't, I launched into a synopsis of the gospel.

I told him that God would have a Day of Justice because He was good by nature. He was going to punish murderers and rapists, but He was so good that He would punish thieves, liars, adulterers, fornicators, etc. Hell was a reality and God didn't want him to go there. He listened intently. I told him that Jesus took his punishment when He was on the Cross. I asked him if he had seen the movie, *The Passion of the Christ*. He had.

"That's what God did for you in Christ."

He nodded and said, "I appreciate the way you presented yourself to me." I had just told him that he was on his way to Hell, and that his beliefs were wrong, and yet he was appreciative. This was because I simply used the Law to bring the knowledge of sin, and his conscience had affirmed the truth of the Commandments. We shook hands and parted.

I'm In Missions

I sat in the holding lounge in Madras, typing on my laptop. Suddenly my eyes caught a businessman sitting about ten feet from me. I felt that I should witness to him. The problem was that he wasn't looking my way. I thought of a number of excuses as to why I shouldn't talk to him. He was busy. He probably didn't speak English. I was busy. But if he died in his sins, he would go to Hell. I prayed, "Please make him look my way." He didn't look my way. So I coughed. I coughed loudly and he looked my way. I said, "How are you doing, sir?"

"Very well."

"Are you going to Germany?"

"Singapore."

"Are you a businessman?"

"I'm with Imation."

That was the name of his company, but I thought that he said, "I'm in missions." So I asked, "Are you a Christian?"

"No."

He stood up and handed me his business card. His name was Mani. I felt that I had blown my cover with my, "Are you a Christian?" so I asked, "Are you a Hindu? What happens after a Hindu dies?"

I expected him to say that they were "reborn" through reincarnation, but he instead said, "It's very expensive. You have to buy all sorts of things to make sure the person's soul lives on. My father died four years ago and it cost three thousand U.S. dollars."

"What's going to happen to you after you die?"

He pulled up a chair beside me. "My kids live in the United States. They will come here and look after everything."

"Have you ever had the Christian message explained to you?"

"No."

"The Bible says that after we die, we are judged by God."

"I believe that. I believe in God."

I then took him through the Commandments, using my own testimony and then into the Cross. He was nodding with every word. I then gave him a *What Hollywood Believes* book and CD. He began reading it as we talked, saying, "I agree with this. This is right."

He said, "Wonderful. Wonderful," and we parted with a handshake.

After he had left and I thought about my initial unfounded fears and our ensuing conversation, I wished that I had pressed him more to make things right with God there and then. But I prayed for him after he left, and I had the consolation that he had the book in his hand and was more than likely to continue reading it on his flight.

When I was in India, someone asked me who I found it most difficult to witness to. I said, "My nemeses are businessmen. Men in suits, in their 50s or 60s. Men who are too busy to listen to a little man with a mustache talk about religion."

On the way back, we were held up in Germany. Our flight was delayed and we were stuck in a holding lounge for about two hours. When a woman asked us how long we had been waiting, we began talking. She very kindly gave EZ and me each a button from Idaho, advertising the state. I then gave her a "What Hollywood Believes" CD. Her friend asked if she could have one. Then others in their party were also requesting CDs. I grabbed some Million Dollar Bills and handed them out. Other passengers were intrigued and began requesting them (about 100 tracts were taken by excited passengers). The delay meant that we missed our connection flight, and EZ and I found ourselves on standby. A few minutes later we were on the plane, heading home.

As I was walking down the aisle giving out Million Dollar Bills, I passed two important looking businessmen. Both looked as though they were in their mid-fifties. I looked at my ticket, and sure enough, I was seated between them. One was an insurance broker. He was on his way to California for a business trip. The other was a trial lawyer, heading for Los Angeles for a case. The lawyer was friendly, outspoken, blasphemous, and unashamedly using filthy language in his conversation. He put his earphones on and said that he was going to listen to the pilot conversation during takeoff.

The insurance broker asked what I did for a living. I told him that I wrote Christian books, and his reaction was positive. I thought that it would be difficult to speak to one of them while the other was overhearing the conversation, so with the lawyer preoccupied, I asked, "Do you ever think about what happens after someone dies? Do you believe in Heaven and Hell?"

He said that he did. Then we went through the Good Test. He thought he was a good person, but then admitted to lying, stealing and lust. He smiled and said, "You boxed me in!" I agreed.

"But my church told me that all I needed to do was go to confession."

"That won't help you on Judgment Day, and this is why."

I explained the courtroom scenario and how any judge will not let a devious criminal go simply because he confessed that he did it, was sorry, or wouldn't do the crime again. Rick was his name. He nodded as I spoke. He admitted his own guilt and that he was going to Hell. When he said that it concerned him, I shared the good news of the Cross, and the necessity of repentance and faith—saving faith—trusting alone in Jesus Christ. All this happened before we ever left the ground. I whispered to Rick, "The one on my left hand is going to be the big challenge." Rick smiled as he nodded.

About ten minutes later John, the trial lawyer, began cross-examining me as to what our TV program was about. I said it was a Christian program and that we taught Christians how to share their faith without causing offense. He had more questions—"How do you do that? What do you say? Where do you film it?"

I said, "The best thing I can do is show you what we do. Do you consider yourself to be a good person?"

"Yes."

"I'm going to put you on the stand and cross-examine you." John began to look a little uncomfortable. I reassured him and said, "It'll be okay. All I need is your honesty for three or four questions. Okay?" He nodded.

"Have you ever told a lie?"

"Yes."

"What does that make you?"

"A liar."

"Have you ever stolen anything?"

"Yes."

"What does that make you?"

"A thief."

"Have you ever used God's name in vain?"

There was a slight hesitation. "Yes."

"No need to hesitate. I heard you blaspheme twice since we began talking."

He smiled.

"That's a very serious crime against God—to use His name as a cuss word."

John smiled and said, "You know, I've often asked people if they have ever told a lie. If they say 'No', you've got them. They just lied. If they say 'Yes,' they are admitting to being a liar."

"This one will nail you. Jesus said, 'Whoever looks upon a woman and lusts after her has committed adultery already with her in his heart. Have you ever done that?"

"Yes."

"John, listen to this. By your own admission you are a lying, thieving, blasphemous adulterer at heart. If God was to judge you by the Ten Commandments, would you be innocent or guilty?"

"Guilty."

"Heaven or Hell?"

"Hell."

"Does that concern you?"

He said that it did, so I shared the gospel with him.

Then we talked about what had happened. I said, "That's what we teach on the program. I addressed your conscience, rather than your intellect, the place of argument. The word 'conscience' means 'with knowledge.'"

John was intrigued. He wrote down the name of the show and said that he would watch for it. It was a warm, personable conversation. I thanked him for listening to me, and he expressed gratitude that I had spoken with him. He then became very friendly, giving me unsolicited updates in his strong Chicago accent on what the pilots were saying, and asking questions such as "When did you last swear?"

"Thirty-three years ago."

"Why don't you swear?"

"I don't need to. I can express what I want to say without using filthy language."

I enjoyed chatting with Rick and him. John apologized when he let bad words out of his mouth. That made me smile.

14

My First Trip to Jail

by Kirk Cameron

My heart was beating a little faster and heavier than usual as I drove into the cement parking structure of the Los Angeles Men's Central Jail—the largest jail in America. I met with the chaplain, who escorted me into the cement criminal-holding tank, through security, past kidnappers, rapists, and serial killers, and into his office. I felt that perhaps I had made a very big mistake.

After watching an episode of "The Way of the Master," in which I shared the gospel with some gang members, the jail chaplain asked if I would be willing to preach to some of his "boys." One of the men I had the privilege to meet was a serial killer who suffered from a genetic disorder called "gigantism" (like "Andre the Giant"), which made him continue to grow to very large proportions. He was nicknamed "Monster" by his fellow inmates. He was doing time for murdering four people. I had to enter a maximum security area and wait for Monster to be brought out of his solitary confinement cell. He was huge, handcuffed, and hairy. As he walked toward us, he locked eyes with me and smiled, presumably remembering me from "Growing Pains." The guards told him sit down on the steel bench to which they would chain him for safety.

Monster said his back was hurting him, so he stepped into a steel shower cage, and the guards closed the shower door, locking the handcuffed giant behind another set of bars. Monster shook my hand, which about disappeared into the folds of his enormously meaty mitts, and told me about how he had learned that although he was a murderer waiting to be executed, like Moses, he could be forgiven by God through humble, repentant faith. He seemed genuinely contrite and professed to have surrendered to Christ as Lord and Savior. Monster said he believed that God had evangelistic work for him to do in the jail, and that if he never made it out, that would be okay. We prayed together, with my eyes slightly open, and he laughed as I slipped him a Million Dollar Bill gospel tract to give to the guards.

Shortly after speaking with Monster, I was introduced to about 800 men who had just finished watching a portion of *Left Behind: The Movie* as a recreational activity. They listened quietly as I shared what God had done to save me. Then I pleaded with them to consider the claims of the gospel and where they would spend eternity if they were to stand before God to give account of their lives. I have to admit, I was a little nervous with the fact that 90 percent of these convicts knew who I was, and might be getting out of jail someday soon. One man stood up and began to recite a poem he had written about "making things right with your Maker while there's time." It was a very sobering atmosphere—one I won't soon forget.

As I left "MCJ," I was particularly aware of the big blue sky and the cool outdoor breeze. I felt so thankful to be free. It made me think of our freedom in Christ. In Him, we are free from the Law, free from the prison of sin, and free to live for God. We were guilty, and God sent Jesus. He took our punishment on the Cross, paid our fine, broke the chains that held us captive, and opened the door to eternal life.

"[There is] therefore now no condemnation to those who are in Christ Jesus" (Romans 8:1).

"If therefore the Son shall make you free, you shall be free indeed" (John 8:36).

Foul Mouths, Frogs, and Magic

I was walking quickly along a busy Indiana highway in the dark, trying to get back to my hotel (I was scheduled to speak at a church), when I noticed a lot of commotion coming from the parking lot. There was a pond surrounded by large rocks and about a dozen loud, foulmouthed teenagers. Water was flying everywhere and the young men sounded like a pack of hyenas that had just captured their prey. When I asked them what they were doing, they laughed and showed me. I felt sick. I watched as one kid lifted up another rock to find a big fat frog, and the others hurled rocks at the frog until they killed it.

I returned to my room, but couldn't stay. I marched back out to the frog killers, armed with some Million Dollar Bill tracts, a simple magic trick, and a determination to share the gospel with some heartless souls. This is how it played out:

"Hey, Guys. Did you get any more frogs?"

"Oh, yeah! Lots!"

"You guys look like you need something else to do. Want to see a magic trick?"

"Yeah! Sure!"

"OK, this is how you can make money. Watch carefully as I turn this one dollar bill into a twenty."

"Whoa!! How did you do that? Do that again!"

"How about you guys answering some trivia questions and I'll give you free money?"

"OK! Me first!"

"What's the capital of France?"

"Paris!"

"Here's your dollar. Now, who wants to go for ten?"

"Me! Me!"

Now remember, I'm holding a ten dollar bill, trapped between a pond filled with frog fungus and twelve murderous teenagers with large rocks in their hands. I suddenly pictured myself as a large toad with curly hair about to be stoned.

"OK, which one of you guys considers himself to be a good person?"

"Not me, dude. I kill frogs!" The others cackled.

"OK, you. What's your name?"

"Tyler."

"Tyler if you pass a simple four question test and prove to me you're a good person, you get the money. OK?"

"OK."

"Have you ever lied?"

"Yes."

"Have you ever stolen something? Anything at all?"

"No."

"Ever taken God's name in vain? Used it as a cuss word?"

"Hell yes! G-d d—n!" (Laugh, laugh, laugh)

"Tyler, Jesus said whoever looks upon a woman to lust after her has committed adultery with her already in his heart."

"What's that?"

"Is he serious?"

"Oh, yeah. I learned about that in my health class."

"Have you ever looked with lust?"

"Yes, I have!"

"Listen up, guys. Tyler, by your own admission, you're a liar, a blasphemer, and an adulterer at heart, and you have to face God on Judgment Day. And that's only four of the Ten Commandments. Do you think you'll be innocent or guilty?"

"Guilty."

"Will you go to Heaven or Hell?"

"I'm going to Heaven, dude, because I go to reconciliation, and the priest rubbed that oil on my head!"

"Tyler, try that in a court of law. 'Your honor, I know I broke the law, but I went to reconciliation and a priest rubbed oil on my head.' Would a good judge let you go?"

"No, but that's a judge, that's not God. God forgives *everybody*!"

"So do you think he should let murderers and rapists into Heaven?"

"No. I don't like rapists. They make me feel bad."

"Of course, He shouldn't. God will give them justice and He'll give you justice too if you die tonight. And God's place of punishment is called Hell."

"Then everybody's going to Hell. You're scaring me, dude."

"That's right. Everybody *deserves* to go to Hell. But God is kind and merciful and provided a way for sinners like us to be forgiven and escape Hell. Do you know what God did?"

"What?"

"He sent His son, Jesus Christ to die on the Cross and take the punishment for sin upon Himself. If you will repent and trust in Him, God will forgive you and grant you everlasting life. But Tyler, I can tell by the way you're acting that you don't take this seriously. Unless you turn from your sin, God will give you justice and you're going to end up worse than that frog you just squashed. You've sinned against the One who gave you your life, and you've made yourself His enemy because of your sin. I'm telling you the truth because I care about you guys and I want you to know how to make things right with God before you die."

I then gave each of the boys a Million Dollar Bill tract, went back to my room, and prayed for them. Here's an idea. Ask God to give you an opportunity to proclaim the glorious gospel to someone today. It may be a group of foulmouthed frog killers, or it might be a friend at work. Or your own mother. The point is, jump at the chance to impact their eternity before they croak. Leap to the conscience, and point a Hell-bound sinner to the

Cross. And pray that with God's help, they might find everlasting life.

> *"Be instant in season and out of season ... do the work of an evangelist"(2 Timothy 4:2).*

And ...

> *"Redeem the time ... making the most of every opportunity ... " (Ephesians 5:16).*

15

Guess Who's in Town
by Ray Comfort

Only once in my life have I regretted being married, and that was only for one second. It was when I began to climb down from a high ladder. My wedding ring caught on the top rung, and for an instant I was dangling by one finger. It wasn't a good feeling.

My wife is used to seeing me do such things. So is the staff at our ministry. My son-in-law even wrote a song in which he sings, "When everything is breaking, when everything is shaking, then there's no mistaking ... Ray Comfort's in town." It's a catchy tune and it has couple of dozen verses. Sue even sings it when she sees me dangling from a ladder by my finger.

Not long after I stretched my wedding ring finger, I was driving our van and noticed an elderly man walking along the sidewalk. I immediately thought that he looked as though he was retired, and that he was out for a walk to break the boredom. He was in reality waiting to die ... and if he didn't know the Lord, he would end up in Hell. I felt sickened by such a thought, and decided to give him a copy of *What Hollywood Believes* (I keep a stack in my vehicle). My strategy was that I would drive into the parking lot of our ministry, wait for him to walk past, and then give him the book.

Do you remember the story of the rich man that God Himself called a "fool"? He so prospered that he decided to build bigger barns and then take it easy for the rest of his days. But God said to him, "You fool, this night your soul shall be required of you: then whose shall those things be, which you have provided?" Then Jesus said, "So is he that lays up treasure for himself, and is not rich toward God" (see Luke 12:15-21).

Before Jesus spoke that parable, He warned, "Take heed, and beware of covetousness: for a man's life consists not in the abundance of the things which he possesses."

He wasn't warning of the peril of riches, but about the danger of the sin of covetousness—transgressing the Tenth Commandment. There is nothing wrong with being rich. Abraham was rich (Genesis 13:2), Solomon was rich (1 Kings 10:23), so was Job, Joseph of Arimathea, and Zacchaeus (see Job 1:3, Matthew 27:57, Luke 19:2). The Scriptures say, "Charge them that are rich in this world, that they be not highminded, nor trust in uncertain riches, but in the living God, who gives us richly all things to enjoy" (1 Timothy 6:17). Again, being rich isn't a sin, but being covetous is—because "sin" is transgression of the Law (see 1 John 3:4).

The Bible says, "As a man thinks in his heart, so is he." What do you and I *think* about? What is it that we meditate on most? It is "desire" that determines most of our thought patterns. It should be that the human predicament narrows down what we think about. Imagine a Titanic survivor. He is sitting with a few other survivors in a large mostly empty lifeboat as the great ocean liner heaves and sinks silently beneath the freezing waters of the Atlantic Ocean. The only sounds that break that eerie silence are the unforgettable cries of perishing human beings, pleading to be saved from an icy grave. There's plenty of room in the lifeboat. What then should consume the survivor's thoughts? He should be utterly focused on saving those around him. *Nothing else should matter, compared to the task that is before him.*

The most important day of our life will be the day of our death. Think about that. On that day, nothing else will matter except what we have done for God and where we are going. Our house, car, possessions, and money will mean nothing on that day. We will be leaving time and entering into eternity. Meditate on that breathtaking moment. With the exhale of your last breath, you will leave everything you love. Your wedding ring. Your spouse. Your loved ones. Your vehicle. Your money. Everything. This very night God could say to you, "This night your soul is required of you."

Let such sobering thoughts consume you. Let them drive you to use your time and your life for what matters, to reach out to the unsaved and make a big dent into this sinful world for Jesus Christ.

16

The Sandblaster

by Ray Comfort

As I looked out of the window in my office, I saw a man step out of a truck. There was some sort of strange equipment on the vehicle. As he looked down the alley, he seemed a little mystified. I wasn't sure if it was my own thoughts or the voice of God, but I heard, "Go and witness to him." Just then I realized who he was. He was there to remove some paint. Two days earlier I had called the "Graffiti Hot Line" and asked for some graffiti to be removed off the wall in the alleyway adjacent to our ministry. Someone had spray-painted the word "Thanks" on the wall.

I ran down the stairs, grabbed a paperback version of *What Hollywood Believes,* and walked toward the alley. By then he had found the graffiti and was backing up the truck. As he got out of the vehicle, I had an attack of the DTs. I noticed that he was big, was smoking a cigarette, had tattoos, and was unshaven. His size told me that he was violent by nature. He was probably the school bully, and no doubt he carried that brutal attitude into life, especially towards Christians. By now he was definitely a murderer. His tattoos and the cigarette strengthened my suspicions. His unshaven appearance told me that he was having a very stressful day from the moment he woke up, and he didn't want to be bothered by some Bible-quoting fanatic. This depraved monster would beat me to a pulp, stab me to death, and leave my wretched body in the alley.

I introduced myself and found that his name was Todd. He was warm and friendly. Nice chap. I then asked him about his job. He said that he only removed graffiti on the weekends. Then I watched in amazement as he sandblasted it off the brick wall as though it had been sprayed written with soft peanut butter.

After he had finished, I handed him the book and said, "This is a book I wrote. It's about 124 big-name celebrities and what they believe about the afterlife."

"I've got this book in hardcover. Bought it at a used bookstore. I haven't read it though."

"What do you think happens after someone dies?"

"I don't know."

"Do you believe in Heaven and Hell?"

"Yes."

"Who goes where? Do good people go to Heaven and bad people go to Hell?"

"Yes. I think so."

"Where do you think *you* will go?"

"Heaven?"

"Let me give you a test. This will really help you work it out. Have you ever told a lie?"

"Yes."

"What does that make you?"

"A liar."

"Have you ever stolen anything?"

"No."

"Have you ever used God's name in vain?"

"Yes."

"That's called blasphemy and it's a very serious sin. It's using God's name as a cuss word. This one will nail you to the wall; it did me. Jesus said that whoever looks upon a woman to lust after her has committed adultery already with her in his heart. Have you ever done that?"

"Yes."

"Todd, I'm not judging you. This is by your own admission. You are a lying, blasphemous adulterer at heart. If God judges you by the Ten Commandments, and we've only looked at four, on the Day of Judgment, do you think that you would be innocent or guilty?"

"Guilty."

"Would you go to Heaven or to Hell?"

"Heaven."

"Why?"

"Because there are lots of things that people do that are worse."

"Think of it like this, Todd. You are in a court of law, guilty of rape and murder. The judge asks if you have anything to say before he passes sentence, and you say, 'I know I'm guilty, Judge, but there are plenty of people that have done worse things than me. Look at what Hitler did.' He's going to say, 'What are you talking about? That's got nothing to do with your crime.' If he is a good judge, he's bound by the law to uphold justice and give you what you deserve. If you died right now, and God gave you justice, you would end up in Hell. The Bible says 'All liars will have their part in the Lake of Fire.' Does it concern you that if you died right now, you would go to Hell?"

"Well, yes, it does."

"Do you know what God did for you so that you wouldn't have to go there? He did a wonderful thing for you."

"No, I don't know."

I explained the Cross to him—how God became a human being and suffered and died for the sin of the world, and how He rose from the dead and defeated death. I told him that he had to repent and trust the Savior to be saved. "If you repent and trust Jesus, God will do with all your sins what you did with that graffiti. He will wash you to a point that will be as though you had never sinned. You are like a criminal who has committed a capital crime. You are worthy of death and what comes after that—damnation. But God can let you live because of what Jesus did. When do you think you will get right with God?"

"Soon."

"If you died right now, where would you go?"

"Hell, presumably."

"Don't you think you should get right with God right now?"

"Yes."

"Do you want to pray?"

"Yes, I do."

"You pray within your mind for thirty seconds—confess your sins to God, then I will pray with you."

That's what we did. Right in the alleyway with the motor of his truck still running. I thanked God for Todd being open and honest, and prayed that this day would be a day of change for him, when he surrendered to the God who gave him life. I also asked God's blessing and good health for him and his family. I then opened *What Hollywood Believes* and showed him the back pages of the book, where we had included "Save Yourself Some Pain," which gives principles of Christian growth. He looked at me, shook my hand, and said, "Thanks for praying for me." I then showed him through our ministry, and we parted.

17

Caller, You're On the Air!

by Kirk Cameron

I was live, on the air, in front of millions with the cast of "Growing Pains," doing my dandiest to answer a caller's question, and squeeze in a clear, thirty-second explanation of why I had become a Christian. We were actually there to promote the fact that "Growing Pains" was now on DVD. Once the program was over, I looked for my opportunity. The talk show host went to the restroom and I stationed myself outside the door. When he came out, I grabbed him by the shoulders and said,

"I watch you all the time—especially when you ask a panel of religious leaders your tough questions about God. You seem to be a man hungry for the answers. If you would just give me ten minutes, I'm sure I could clear it all up for you. What do you say?"

"Call me tomorrow at 4:30."

"OK. You got it. 4:30."

What had I done? Now I had the chance to witness to one of the most popular and influential talk show hosts in America and I was going to do it on the phone? I thought to myself, "If only there was a way to get into his office." The next day, I called at 4:30.

(Ring, ring.)

"Hello?"

"Hi, it's me—Kirk—calling you back at 4:30, like you asked. Thanks so much for taking my call."

"Kirk, would you like to come into my office and talk about this?"

"When?"

"Monday. 4:30. Eleventh floor."

"I'll be there. Monday. 4:30. Eleventh floor. See you then."

I could hardly believe it! I didn't even have to ask him. He invited me into his office to talk about the things of God! I took a deep breath and exhaled slowly. The weekend passed and Monday came. I was at the office early. I drove around the building several times, praying for God's help in the meeting. I parked and went to the 11th floor. I knocked on the door and a different, secret, unmarked door opened instead. I was escorted into the waiting room. The walls were covered with pictures of the host and the president of the United States, Paul McCartney, Colin Powell, and just about every religious leader, politician, and entertainer I could think of at that moment. What was I doing here? Why in the world did he want *me* to talk with him about God? What could I say that he hasn't heard before?

I could see him through the glass wall of his office, reclining on his red chaise, watching the news with one of his producers. He motioned me in, sat me down, and gave me a piece of Oreo cookie cheesecake. I wasn't hungry; I was too nervous. He said to me in his deep, gravelly voice, "So, what can Kirk Cameron do for me?"

"Well, I'm sure I can't do anything for you, but I think you ask great questions and many of your guests never want to give you straight answers because they are afraid of offending their audience. I'd like to answer them and explain to you why I was an atheist who became a Christian."

"Let me just tell you, I'm Jewish. I used to believe in God, but somewhere along the way I lost it, and have never been able to find it again. The thought that there is a God out there, watching me … is a riot. I think that's hilarious!"

"I understand. I used to be an atheist myself. But I know how to prove that God exists in two minutes without even mentioning faith or the Bible. Would you like me to show you? It will really help."

"Go ahead."

I gave him the classic proof of creation to prove the existence of God. He smiled and asked another question.

"OK, then who made God?"

"That's another good question. The answer will hurt your brain; are you sure you want it?"

"Give it to me."

I explained how the observation of space, because it appears to have no beginning or end, causes scientists to believe that it is eternal—never ending. This gives us a glimpse of the eternity of God, who *created* space. If space and time are dimensions God created and He dwells outside of them, then God doesn't require a beginning or end either. God didn't "start." He always was. Nobody made God. He is eternal.

We went back and forth. He asked his usual rapid-fire questions about why God lets children die of cancer, why some people get wiped out by a hurricane like Katrina and others don't. He said that whoever invented religion was a genius because it is the perfect way to control and manipulate masses of people. He even told me that Judas was the real hero of the gospels, because "Jesus would never have become famous if it wasn't for Judas. Every good story needs to have a villain. Without Judas, Jesus wouldn't have a story! I think it's sad that more parents don't name their children 'Judas'."

Then I turned the tables and asked him a question: "Would you consider yourself to be a good Jew?"

"I'm a *very* good Jew."

"Do you think you've kept the Law of Moses—the Ten Commandments?"

"No."

"Have you ever lied?"

"Yes."

"What does that make you?"

"An occasional liar."

"Have you ever stolen anything—regardless of the value?"

"Yes. But I returned it."

"What does that make you?"

"A one-time thief."

"Have you ever taken the name of God in vain?"

"Sure."

"That's called blasphemy. You've taken the name of the One who's given you your life and everything that is precious to you and used it as a replacement for a four-letter filthy word to express disgust. Not even Hitler, who murdered six million innocent Jews, is so despised today that his name is used as a filthy curse word, but you've used God's name that way. Last question. A famous rabbi said that whoever looks upon a woman to lust after her has committed adultery with her already in his heart. Have you ever looked with lust?"

"Many times."

"Listen to this. By your own admission, you're a lying thief and a blasphemous adulterer at heart, and you have to face God on Judgment Day. If God judges you according to the Ten Commandments, will you be innocent or guilty?"

"Guilty."

"Does that mean you're going to Heaven or Hell?"

"I don't believe in either."

"That doesn't matter. Please don't walk into the street with an eighteen-wheeler headed toward you and say you don't believe in traffic. You'll get crushed! Your lack of belief doesn't change reality. If God is good, He will punish lawbreakers and that means you're in trouble whether you believe in God or not. The Scriptures say that all liars will have their part in the

Lake of Fire, and that no thief, no adulterer, no blasphemer will inherit the Kingdom of Heaven. If God gives you justice, you won't be headed for Heaven, but for His place of punishment called Hell. And by the way, you don't go there just because you 'don't believe in Jesus.' You'll go to Hell *because you've sinned against God.*"

While it may seem like I laid a very heavy weight upon his shoulders, it was obvious to me that he needed to see himself in truth from God's perspective, and perceive his sin problem. Only then would he be able to appreciate the solution in Christ. Besides, if I didn't tell this famous man about his sin and the coming Judgment, who would tell him?

We then talked about the love of God, demonstrated 2000 years ago at Calvary's Cross. I opened the floodgates of Scripture to show him how deep, and wide, and long, and high is the love of God toward all who repent and trust in the Savior. I told him how he could be forgiven for all his sins and be reconciled to God through faith in Jesus, and pass from death to life ... be born again, a new man in Christ.

After an hour of conversation, this professional questioner thanked me, shook my hand, stood up, and said, "I have to do a show now. I enjoyed this. You can come back on my show anytime," and walked out.

I put my fork and plate of cheesecake down on the desk, turned to the producer— he had been in the room the whole time, quiet as a mouse behind his computer screen—and witnessed to him. By the end of our meeting, I was exhilarated. Needless to say, my drive home was filled with prayer. Prayers bursting with gratitude for being used by God to proclaim the glorious gospel to an "untouchable," and prayers that the famous man with all the questions would come to the knowledge of the truth and be saved. I couldn't stop smiling. It had been a *very* good day.

18

Oops! Wrong Taxi Driver

by Ray Comfort

The phone awoke me at 4:30 a.m. I showered, dressed, and then made my way down for the 5:10 a.m. hotel shuttle to the Denver airport. I gave the lady at the desk a Million Dollar Bill tract, and waited outside for the shuttle to arrive.

As I sat down, a man in his mid 20s who had followed me out of the hotel asked me for a tract. It was 5:00 a.m. and I really didn't feel like witnessing. I gave him a tract and said, "It's a gospel tract. Do you know what a gospel tract is?'

"No."

"It's about what happens after you die. Where do you think people go to?"

"Heaven or Hell."

"Where do you think you will go to?"

"Heaven, I hope."

"Do you think you are a good person?"

He hesitated, and said, "Yes."

"What's your name?"

"Peter."

Peter was from the Ukraine, but his English was easy for me to understand despite his heavy accent. I took him through the Commandments and, of course, he proved to be a lying, thieving, lust-filled blasphemer.

"Do you think that you will go to Heaven or Hell?"

"Hell."

"Does that concern you?"

"Yes, it does."

"Do you know what God did for you so that you wouldn't go to Hell?"

Peter obviously had a Christian background because he then talked about the Cross, repentance, and faith in Jesus.

"When do you think that you will get right with God?"

He hesitated to answer.

"If you died right now, where would you go?"

"Hell."

"Shouldn't you get right with God today? Now?"

Peter then said, "Today is the day of salvation." Then he repeated the verse.

I gave him a *What Hollywood Believes* book and CD. Just then, a taxi driver came over to us. I also gave him a Million Dollar Bill tract and a CD, and did a little sleight of hand for them both. The taxi driver loved it, then went back to his vehicle.

I talked with Peter again about getting right with God that day, and how death can snatch us at any time. Then I did a little more magic (sleight of hand) and decided to wave the taxi driver back for some more early morning entertainment. As he got out of the car, I realized that it was a *different* taxi driver—the first one must have taken off with a customer when I was talking to Peter. He walked over with a rather mystified expression on his face. I did some magic, which he loved, gave him a CD, and he went back to his vehicle.

I waited until 5:22 a.m. The super-shuttle was super-late, so I decided that I had better get a taxi rather than miss my flight. I waved to my new friend; he jumped out, grabbed my bags, put them in the trunk, and we were off to the airport.

"What's your name?"

"Housan."

"Where are you from?"

"Somalia."

"What's this pamphlet? It looks like Hebrew."

"It's Arabic."

In front of me was an Islamic tract, presumably placed so that Arabic-speaking passengers would see it.

"Where do you think you will go when you die?"

"I hope to go to Heaven. I will have to wait until I die to see."

"What if you don't make it?"

"I don't know. I ask God to forgive me all the time." Housan then changed the subject a little. He remarked, "Islam is a peaceful religion."

"But what about Jihad? If I'm an infidel, don't you have to kill me?"

"No. Whoever does that is not a Moslem. We believe in Jesus. He was a prophet. I believe in Jesus more than you do. We believe in Moses also."

I knew that I had at least 30 minutes to take him through the Law, so I decided to make a very important point before doing so.

"What would you think if a man raped and murdered a woman and then said to the judge, 'Judge, I'm really sorry about what I did. I won't do it again, so you can let me go'?"

Housan laughed and said that the judge would *never* let him go. He had to be punished.

"That's right. If the judge is good, he has to make sure that justice is done, that the man is punished."

"Yes."

"Have you heard of the Ten Commandments?"

"No."

"That was the Law that God gave to Moses. You shall not lie, steal, kill or commit adultery."

"Yes, that's right. It's wrong to do those things."

"Housan. Have you ever lied?"

"Yes, when I was younger."

"So that makes you a liar. Have you ever stolen anything?"

"No. That's one thing I wouldn't do. Someone left a bag in my taxi once. I didn't even open it, and the owner gave me a $500 reward when I returned it."

"Have you ever used God's name in vain?'

"What do you mean?"

"Have you said, "Oh, my G-d! or G-d this or that?"

"Yes, I have done that. Is it wrong?"

"Yes. It's using God's name as a cuss word, and it's called 'blasphemy.' It's *very* wrong. Jesus said, 'You have heard it said You shall not commit adultery, but I say to you, whoever looks upon a woman to lust after her has committed adultery already with her in his heart.' Have you ever looked at a woman with lust ... with sexual desire?"

For the next few minutes Housan tried to justify himself. He first pleaded ignorance as to what I meant by *desiring* a woman. After some vivid explanations of what I meant, he finally admitted to lusting after women.

"So, Housan, by your own admission, you are a lying, blasphemous adulterer at heart. What's going to happen to you on Judgment Day? God can't let you go just because you are sorry and you won't do it again. He must punish you because He is good. You will end up in Hell."

He didn't try to justify himself, so I then shared the Cross with him, and the necessity of repentance and faith. I labored the fact that his fine was paid by God in Christ.

He asked, "What do you think will happen to Moslems?"

"*Anyone* who dies without Christ as their Savor will be guilty before God and end up in Hell. *Anyone.*"

He the asked, "How many wives can a Christian have?"

"Not more than seventy."

Housan laughed out loud. "You're funny. Thank you for talking to me."

As we parked at the Denver airport, I gave him a good tip, a *What Hollywood Believes* book, and prayed with him—that God would reveal the Cross to him, confirm the truth of what I had said, and continue to bless him and his family with health.

Back in LA

As I got into the taxi at Los Angeles International Airport I handed a Million Dollar Bill tract to the driver. He also had a deep accent and said, "What's this?"

I said, "It's a million dollars. It's yours." He laughed, grabbed my bags, and got into the driver's seat.

"What's your name?"

"Mark."

He had a plain name for such a deep accent.

"Where are you from?"

"Ukraine."

"Mark, what do you think happens when someone dies? Where do they go to?"

"Fertilizer. Dirt."

"You don't believe in Heaven and Hell?"

"No. That's all #@&*%$! What about those twenty-seven children that were killed last night! What about them?"

I had no idea what he was talking about, so I said, "Whose fault was that? Sinful men."

Mark seemed to see my point, and then he said, "What about America? So filled with greed. Bill Gates has %$#!* billions and he wants more. Billions! People want bigger houses. Do you have a car? You want a better one!"

As Mark spoke, he eyes flashed with anger. He was clenching his huge fists and raising his deep voice in an almost demonic rage. "Fat. They are so fat. Eat, #@*&$! eat, eat."

"So how are things in the Ukraine?"

"People are just the same there!"

"Sinful hearts are everywhere, Mark. All humanity has sinned. We need to get you a soapbox, because you are preaching Bible."

His accent was so strong and his demeanor so angry that I decided not to take him through the Law.

As we pulled up outside of my house, I paid him, gave him a generous tip, and said, "Do you read much?"

"Yes, I do."

"Well you stay there. I'll get my bags out. Then I want to give you a book I wrote."

I grabbed my bags before he could get to them and rushed inside.

Mark was standing by his vehicle when I came out. I gave him a copy of *The Mystery*, a gripping novel that thoroughly uses the Law to bring the knowledge of sin. I signed the book and handed it and a "What Hollywood Believes" CD to him. He smiled from ear to ear.

As I walked back to the house, he said, "God bless you. God bless you."

He held the book up in his big hands and said, "You make my day ... you make my day."

Speedy Taxi

Kirk and I were due to fly to Tennessee to speak at a conference. We were leaving the airport on a 6:00 a.m. flight, and I was leaving my home at 4:30 a.m. The taxi driver got out of his car as I approached it.

"Hi, I'm Ray."

"Huh?"

"I'm Ray. What's your name?"

"Huh?"

"Me Ray. You?"

"Oh. Orlando."

Here was one taxi driver I wouldn't be witnessing to, but as I sat in the back seat of the car, Orlando was able to understand what I meant by "turn left, and "turn right," so I decided I would give it a try:

"Orlando. Do you read your Bible?"

"Huh?"

"Do you read the Bible?'

"I no understand. Speaka Spaneesh?"

I didn't, but I decided I would let him know how little I spoke by saying the only two words I knew. I blurted out:

"Bueno Pronto!"

He didn't answer or even say another word for twenty minutes as he raced to the airport like a madman, driving at times between 75 and 80 m.p.h.

As we sped to the airport I realized what I had said to him: "Good. Fast!" I would have told him that I wasn't in a hurry, but decided that I had already put my foot in my mouth and would probably only make things worse. The poor man even printed out a receipt before we arrived at the airport and jumped out of the car the second it stopped to help me grab my luggage.

Understandably, I beat Kirk to the airport. When he arrived, we handed tracts to the attendant at the counter, and Kirk explained that he had lost his wallet and consequently his driver's license while he was in Florida a week or so earlier. However, he had been given paperwork from the DMV, giving him some sort of identity information. The female attendant smiled and said that he should expect a "date" and he went through the security department.

They were all over Kirk as he went through security, so I decided that I would go ahead, get him a cup of coffee, and meet him at the gate.

After about twenty minutes of waiting, I called him and found that airport police were holding him. It turned out that a few months earlier, a brother who loved "The Way of the Master" TV program had given him a 1941 live bullet that he had found on the beach as a reminder that Kirk was fighting a battle. Kirk had dropped it into his bag and forgotten about it—until security found it and decided to interrogate him.

I waited for another ten minutes at the gate and then watched as our flight began boarding. I decided that I would go back to security to give him his coffee and some moral support. I figured he would need it.

I spotted Kirk surrounded by police. So I walked up to him and reached out the coffee. Kirk quickly said, "You had better go back, Ray!" The police weren't so polite. They beckoned with their hands and said firmly, "Get back, sir! Now!"

I quickly backed out of the area and moved back to a counter where two other officers were sitting and said, "Hi. Have you heard of Kirk Cameron?"

The male officer on the right said that he hadn't. The female said that the name sounded familiar, and nodded some more when I said, "Kirk was in the sitcom 'Growing Pains' for seven years. He lost his wallet and has no ID. He had a bullet in his bag, and he's now being held for interrogation."

The male officer spat out, "What's your point?"

"Um … our flight is boarding. Can you let him go?"

"No!"

I decided that I would go back to the gate and wait for Kirk there before I was arrested.

I approached the attendant at the gate and went through the "Do you know Kirk Cameron" scenario again. She did, so I thought that she might say, "Oh, I love Kirk Cameron. I will call the plane and let them know what's going on. They will hold the flight until Kirk arrives." Instead, she informed me that the door to the plane was closing in two minutes. At that point, I decided that I wouldn't board if Kirk didn't arrive.

Suddenly I spotted him running toward us. They had run a background check on him; he had come up clean; and they had released him despite the fact that he had a two-edged sword in his bag.

The brother who kindly issued Kirk with the live ammunition was right about fighting a battle. Thanks to him, we sure were in the middle of one, and we hadn't even left L.A.

Kirk left the conference a day earlier than I did, and I found myself alone, passing through Dallas airport on the way back to Los Angeles. During the flight I wrote down my experience with Orlando the speedy taxi driver, and then read from a book by a lady named "Sandi." I sat down in the Dallas airport and began listening to a pod cast of "The Way of the Master Radio." After about ten minutes, a woman asked me if she could sit in the seat beside me. I said I would be happy for her to sit there, and asked her name and where she was from. Her name was Sandi and she was from Orlando. I said that I co-hosted a Christian TV show and asked her if she had a Christian background. She was Roman Catholic and she thought that she was a good person. I ignored the fact that she had told me that she was a Roman Catholic and simply took her through the Good Test. It was a very typical witnessing encounter. I left her with a pocket *Evidence Bible* and a copy of the "What Hollywood Believes" CD, and felt that the meeting had truly been a divine encounter.

The flight was delayed so I went and purchased something to eat and plunked down on another seat to indulge myself. After a few minutes a gentleman sat two seats away from me. He was tall. That showed me he hated Christians. He had a computer on his lap. That confirmed that he was an intellectual, pro-gay, liberal, save-the-earth, hug-the-trees, raging evolutionist! I felt like quickly moving away because obviously he would murder me if I tried to witness to him.

I ignored my fears and asked, "How are you?"

"Good."

"What do you do for a job?"

"I'm a facial plastic surgeon."

"Does that really work? Or do you end up with a face that won't work because it's stiff?"

"It depends on what work is done."

135

"I have a gift for you. It's what Hollywood celebrities believe about the afterlife. It's really interesting. What do you think happens when someone dies?"

"I hope they go to a better place."

"Heaven?"

"Kind of."

"Will you go there? Do you consider yourself to be a good person?"

"I know I am."

He turned out to be a lying, thieving adulterer at heart. Then he said, "But I still think that I would still go to Heaven."

"Do you know what you've now done?"

"What?"

"You did what I did before I was a Christian. You broke the First and the Second of the Ten Commandments by making a god in your own image, a god you feel comfortable with. But the God of the Bible is perfect, Holy, just, and good ... He will by no means clear the guilty. All liars will have their part in the Lake of Fire. No thief or adulterer will enter the Kingdom of God. Think about why I'm talking to you like this. It's only because I care about you and your family— where you spend eternity. Oops, got to run—my flight is boarding. Make sure you listen to the CD. Thanks for listening to me. Nice to meet you."

19

Witnessing to Scott P.
(A Maximum Security Prisoner)

Written by a prison guard who wanted to remain anonymous

S cott is a prisoner in the AC—the hole of holes, the Adjustment Center of a Maximum Security Prison in California. I worked there last week and that was the first time I saw him. He is pretty thin, looks like he is fifteen to twenty pounds lighter than some pictures on TV that I have seen, and he is in a very humble state of life. At that time the first thing that came to my mind was that I might have an opportunity to share "The Way of the Master" with him. It is like throwing dice to see if you can talk with Scott. There are only seventy cages per yard, to be shared with 100 plus inmates, so you don't know when and who will be out on the yard on any given day. Plus we are so busy, he is out there for about an hour and a half, and I have a partner that must be willing to go over to him with me so I can talk with him. Well, the opportunity did not happen. My wife and friends told me, "God will give you another time," and I agreed with them.

Well, last Sunday night I called my work to see where I would be working, and they said the AC. I told my wife that I was going to share the gospel with Scott on Monday, even though I really didn't know for sure.

I went to work, got assigned to the AC yard, and looked on the list, but Scott's name wasn't there. Then we found out that the computers crashed last night and they printed a new list, and his name was on the new list! I then prayed and told God that I was going to make the most of this opportunity. God in His grace and mercy blessed him to hear the full gospel.

As an officer, I try not to show favoritism or show that I am reaching out to one specific inmate. So as we were running the seventeen inmates back into their houses inside, I didn't say anything more to Scott. He did reach out to me one last time by asking me, "If God is so loving and He sent Jesus to save us, then why did He only send Him to one group of people in one location of the world?"

I quickly told him, "You need to pray and read the Bible and God will answer you. But here is a quick answer—that was God's plan. He was going to bring His Salvation through one nation, the Jews, as a witness to the whole world. You *need* to read the Bible, Scott."

And that was the end, but the beginning of many opportunities to come!

The best way that works for me so far in witnessing has been this line, "Hello, could you help me with my homework?" A lot of people want to help, so most say, Yes. Then I say, "I took a "Way of the Master" class at my church, and for our homework we have to ask some fun questions of people." Some say okay or ask what kind of questions since they already know that I am a churchgoing person, but the fun begins when you ask them, "Would you consider yourself to be a good person?"

I usually give them the shorter version and then at the end I give them my homework sheet, so they can contact me and have God's Word to read for themselves. Any beginner can do this because on this homework assignment, you can use cheat notes!

The biggest thing that I love about "The Way of the Master" is when people leave after talking with you, they do not think about you—they leave totally thinking about God and what His Word says about their afterlife and death.

One last story about Scott P. At the prison we have over 620 death-row inmates. About six weeks ago, I worked in the East Block, which is a very large unit—five levels tall with over 500 hundred inmates. I worked for a month on level 3-Bayside, which is all condemned inmates.

I got to know two inmates that are on fire for Christ and are God's main witnesses there. They have scheduled their own times of worship, prayer, testimonies, and Bible studies. They ministered to me several times to the point that I had to hide the tears that quickly filled my eyes. Well, I shared "The Way of the Master" with them, they copied my homework and now the full gospel is being shared in the deep, dark places where there seems to be no light.

God is so good, and when Scott P. settles into his final home, the seeds that have been planted will be watered by the true living waters. Plus if he gets a home in the original death row— the penthouse of the prison— Administrative Segregation, I know that there are strong Christian inmates there that will continue to witness to him and God will answer all his questions.

20

Witnessing to
Jim Carrey

by Ray Comfort

In November 2004, actor Jim Carrey appeared on CBS's "Sixty Minutes" talking about his belief in God. I had included his spiritual views in *What Hollywood Believes* and decided to tape the program. We were at the time considering approaching the major TV networks with a pitch for a program based on the book.

As we watched the CBS interview, my heart broke for him. He was unashamed to say that he took strength from the spiritual side of his life, and those who didn't like that he expressed strong spiritual beliefs would just have to deal with it. When you are being paid more than $20,000,000 per movie, you don't really care what any producer thinks. *Big* stars can let their light shine without any fear of dark and negative repercussions. I had never seen any actor so bare his soul. When the interviewer coldly said, "You are *very* emotional." Jim responded with "Yeah. I've decided to be there. I only act in the movies."

Three months later, I was told that a young lady I had never met, named Kelsey Johnson, had witnessed to him. She saw him at a yogurt store in Malibu and spoke to him about the things of God. I contacted her and asked her for the details. This is what she said:

At 9:30 p.m. on Wednesday, March 6, 2005, I got this crazy craving for Malibu Yogurt. I go to school at Pepperdine University in Malibu, California. I'm in there and I see him walk in. I'm from a super small town in Minnesota where there are six thousand people, and the biggest celebrity I've even seen is our mayor.

I turned around and said, "Lord, that's Jim Carrey. No, it's not. I'm in Malibu ... yes, it is. What do I do? Do I witness to him?" I heard your message on "What Hollywood Believes" and I was really burdened for Bruce Willis and Jim Carrey. I said, "Okay, God, this is completely divine. What do I do?" I felt like Jeremiah. I didn't know what to do, so I left (like an idiot), got into my car, and drove around the block. I drove around the block three times, praying, "God, do you want me to go back?" I felt that God was saying to me, "You can't speak, but I can, so let me use you."

I parked my car in the parking lot and sat there for another five minutes, and by this time, he was outside. I was sure that he would have left. He was sitting at a table with a couple of kids sitting with him. I thought that I would go up to him and ask, "Did you get one of these?" I would give him a tract and then go from the natural to the supernatural.

So I go up to him, and there's a guy from Pepperdine who I'd never seen before, and he's talking to him about God already. I thought, "Okay, this is nice. I hope he knows Scripture and that he's going to go through the Law with him, and judgment, and why we need a Savior."

So I went up and just butted into the conversation and said, "Hi, I'm Kelsey,"

"I'm Jim."

"So you guys are talking about God. That's real interesting. I heard something about you."

"Oh no."

"You know Ray Comfort?"

"No."

"Do you know Kirk Cameron?"

"Yeah, I know Kirk"

"He's in a ministry called Living Waters, and Ray Comfort wrote a book called *What Hollywood Believes,* and you're in it. I heard that you believed in God. What does that mean to you?"

Jim pushed his yogurt to the side. It was so awesome to see that he wanted to talk. He wasn't freaked out.

I asked, "What does a relationship with God mean to you."

"I believe that there's a God. I look around and I know that there's a God. There's got to be a Creator."

"Do you understand that there's more?"

The guy that was talking to him was saying that Jim had the right idea, but I wanted to let him know that the concept that he had of God wasn't biblical. He thought that we are in Hell right now.

"If you died tonight where do you think that you would go?"

"I'd like to think that I would go to Heaven. I'd like to think that I'd go to a better place."

"What is Heaven to you?"

"I think it's a place where you are happy."

I said, "The Bible says that Hell is not going to be a good time."

"The most important thing that you can do on this earth is be happy with yourself. I don't really like to think too much about what happens when you die. I'm finally at a place now where I understand who God is."

"What do you think about 'sin'?"

"I think that we are born good."

"What do you think that the Bible means when it says that there is not one righteous. Not one."

He asked, "Where does it say that? ... I'm not quite sure." He had his hand on his chin. He was so humble. It was wonderful. So I told him, and he said, "Wow," like it really got him thinking. I asked him if he thought that all roads lead to Heaven, or if he thought that there was one way.

"I think that people will find God; that there is more than one way to Heaven."

I asked him what Jesus meant when He said that He was the way, the truth and the life, and that no one comes to Father except through Him.

"Jesus spoke in parables. I think that He spoke metaphorically. If I saw 'John' walking into a store, I wouldn't say that *John* is the way to the store. I would say that the door is."

"Jim, Jesus also said He's the Door. He's the only way to Heaven. If you say you know God but you don't know Jesus, you don't know God because Jesus is God. That's what the Bible says."

Then we moved on to the topic of Jesus. He separated Jesus and God. He thought that Jesus was a cool guy, and the Bible talks highly of Him, and he said, "But I worship God."

So I asked, "Would you call yourself a good person?"

"I think I'm good."

"Do you think that your goodness will get you to Heaven?"

"Yes."

"On Judgment Day you will have to face the God who gave you life. The Bible says that if you look with lust after a woman, you commit adultery of the heart. Now that's heavy. That's a daily thing for people. That's sin in God's eyes, and the wages of sin is death."

He didn't really want to go there. He knew a few parables and a few Psalms. He didn't know about Hell or about judgment. Hopefully he does now. I said that if you told one lie, even if a tiny white lie, that's sin. He didn't know what to say. I'm praying that he was cut to the heart.

I said, "Don't just take what I'm saying, go to the Bible and read it for yourself. Jim, this has been a great conversation, and I pray you seek the Lord."

He said, "I've enjoyed this." He was really nice about it.

Afterwards I said, "Lord, that was fully You." Six months ago I thought I was a Christian and I was preaching, "You've got a God-shaped hole in your heart"—a selfish message that creates backsliders. I can see how God's timing has worked out, because I was able share the Law and why we need a Savior. I couldn't sleep that night.

21

Don't Back Down

by Ray Comfort

Years ago a delightful picture spread across the Internet. It was a stork swallowing a tenacious frog. The frog was halfway down the bird's throat, but its little hands were tightly wrapped around the stork's neck. As long as the frog held on, the bird couldn't swallow him. Across the top were the words, "Never Give Up!"

We need to have the same attitude when it comes to witnessing to the unsaved. Death wants to swallow them and take them to Hell, and with God's help we must be tenacious both in prayer and with the gospel. Don't let go while the unsaved are still in this life.

Recently I spoke to a man named "Claudio." He was delivering DVDs to our ministry, so I said, "Do you know what you are delivering?" He didn't.

"They are Christian DVDs. Do you have a Christian background?"

He said that he didn't, and that he didn't like to talk about God. He said that he was "up to here with God" as he gestured over the top of his head with his hand. I could have easily eased off at that point and felt that I had done my best to speak to him, but instead I asked what he thought happens after death.

He said that he didn't care. That was another point where I could have given up. He said that he had had it with God and didn't care about where he went when he died. So in good conscience I could have changed the subject. But I didn't. I said, "I'm sure that you really do care. Do you think that you are a good person?"

He did. So I quickly went through four of the Commandments and found that he admitted to lying, blaspheming, and lusting "all the time."

"Would you be innocent or guilty on the Day of Judgment?"

"Guilty."

"Would you go to Heaven or to Hell?"

He immediately said, "I would go straight to Hell."

I told him that I would hate that to happen to him. I could see from his facial expression that such a thought really did concern him.

I continued, "Do you know what God did for you so that you wouldn't have to go to Hell? He did something wonderful for you. Jesus took your punishment upon Himself when He died on the Cross."

He seemed to miss what I was trying to say, and began to tell me that when he was in the military, God protected him in battle. Then he said, "I have made peace with my God."

I questioned, "How did you do that? How did you make peace with God?"

He then told me that he had killed people. Lots of people. He said that when he killed his first, it sickened him. Then it became easy. He said that he had fought in South America and in Iraq.

He said, "When the military hits a building with precision, that doesn't just 'happen.' I grew a beard and long hair, looked like them, dressed like them, and ate like them. I was there for seven months. My unit put 'homing' devices in those buildings. I have killed many people and I have prayed to God about it."

He was awkward in his speech as he tried to explain what he meant in that he had made peace with God. It was obvious that he was riddled with guilt, and that even though he had prayed, he didn't know what to do to get rid of his guilt.

I gave Claudio a signed copy of *What Hollywood Believes* and a CD of the same name, and thanked him for listening to me. He was enthusiastic as he said that he read a lot, and would read it and listen to the CD. As he bent down from the truck deck to shake my hand, I asked if I could pray for him. As we held hands and prayed, he knelt on one knee. I asked God to speak to him through the book, heal all his pains, and bless him and his family with health.

May God make us as desperate as that little frog. His very life was at stake, and that's why he held on with such tenacity. When we witness to the lost, it's their lives that are in danger, not ours. May the love of God cause each of us to be as concerned and as tenacious as if it were our lives that were in terrible danger.

Mysterious Ways

I was pretty exhausted after a full weekend of ministry. Kirk, Duane Barnhart, our producer, and I had flown from L.A. to Chicago and then to Springfield, and then had driven to Branson, Missouri for a conference. After the conference we had the great joy of preaching the gospel (open-air style) inside a mall to hundreds of people.

Afterwards, I interviewed a man who was holding a large white duck. As the interview unfolded I found out that he was a professional comedian. He said, "How would you like to shake hands with a duck?" I immediately reached out and shook hands with the bird. Then he said, "Have you ever shaken hands with a duck before?"

"No."

"You still haven't. That was his foot."

I was then driven back to Springfield, flew from Dallas to Houston, from Houston to Memphis, and then from Memphis back to Los Angeles. So it was understandable that on the flight to L.A., I was exhausted. However, I couldn't sleep because I was in the insomniac row of the plane. The very back row is the one in which the seats don't go back. Besides, the lady next to me had a toddler on her lap and the little cutie tended to scream if I wasn't pulling faces, doing sleight of hand, or making weird noises with my mouth.

After three hours of magic, face-pulling, and intermittent writing, I decided to get up and give the flight attendant a copy of *What Hollywood Believes*. She was excited and showed the book to a man who was sitting across the aisle from me. That gave me an opportunity to try and witness to him. As he was fingering through the publication, I passed him a copy of the CD of the same name. He asked what the book and CD were about, so I told him that they were about Hollywood celebrities and what they believed about the afterlife. I then asked him what he thought happens after death. He didn't answer with much enthusiasm, and the sound of the engines tended to kill any meaningful conversation. So I decided to change gears a little. I told him that I co-hosted a TV program with Kirk Cameron—where we go to the streets and ask people questions about the afterlife. Then I asked what he did for a living. He said that he was a movie and television producer, so I asked him if he would like for me to mail him his own copy of the book. He said that he would, and handed me his business card.

The next day I typed his name and address onto a label. His name was Jim, so I thought that I would sign the book to personalize it. It would say, "To Jim, with best wishes. Yours, Ray." Then I would put my personal email address under that (something I rarely give out) in case he wanted to talk further about the possibility of doing a television program based on the book, something I had been praying about.

I walked into our store and grabbed a hard cover copy of the book off of a pile. I then walked back to my office, sat down, and opened it at the title page. I was about to write "To Jim, with best wishes. Yours, Ray" and then write my email address when I saw something I could hardly believe. There, written in my own handwriting were the words I hadn't yet written—"To Jim, with best wishes. Yours, Ray." Underneath it was my personal email address! It was *exactly* what I was about to write. I was mystified. Dumbfounded.

A moment later I realized what had happened. Two weeks earlier I had sent three signed copies to Jim Carrey at three different addresses, hoping that at least one would get to him. This particular book had been returned by UPS, and mistakenly had been put back into the store. That was the copy I had picked up.

I thought that perhaps this was God's way of letting me know that He was leading me. It *was* encouraging, but before I entered into anything with Hollywood, I wanted to know that I *really* did have God's leading. So I sent the book through the Post Office. If he actually received it, it would be an *obvious* miracle.

When you're a Christian, mysterious things do happen. Sometimes it might be coincidental; other times God proves to have a hand in an incident. My friend Mark Spence (the Dean of our School of Biblical Evangelism) once saw that someone had called his cell phone. He didn't recognize the number, so he hit "redial." When he recognized the voice of one of his friends, he said, "What's up?"

His friend said, "*You* called me."

Mark has a rather strange sense of humor so he answered, "Why didn't you tell me?"

"Tell you what?"

"Oh, is that how's it going to be, huh? Whatever, man. I know what you did."

"You do?"

"Why didn't you tell me? I thought we were friends."

"How did you find out?"

"Oh, come on. God knows everything."

"What do you know?"

At this point Mark was still fooling around. He continued, "I know everything, man. Do you need to talk?"

"It's eating me up. I don't know what to say."

He suddenly realized that his twisted sense of humor had him in hot water. He asked, "Have you told anybody?"

"No, I haven't told anybody."

"What are you going to do about it?"

"What should I do?"

"I think you should tell the pastor."

At this point, Mark still had no idea what his friend had done.

His friend said, "I don't know what I'm going to do."

He had committed adultery.

22

Enterprise

by Ray Comfort

Our van had been dinged, and I rented a car for nine days while it was being repaired. After it was fixed, I was surprised as I entered the car rental place to return the vehicle. There are usually people sitting around, waiting to pick up or drop off cars. Each person in the room usually meant extra time I would have to spend waiting. But this day, no one was there except five workers and myself. As I approached the counter, a young man dressed in a smart suit said, "I'm Dennis," and stretched out his hand to shake mine. I shook his hand and held out my wallet, showed a picture of my stretched head and simply said, "ID." There was a roar of laughter from behind the desks. Dennis was a little surprised, but also laughed. For the next five minutes I ran through my routine. I gave him a Million Dollars and told him he was doing a good job. More laughter. Then I gave him my "Department of Annoyance" card, showed him other pictures in my wallet, and did some sleight of hand. That impressed him.

After filling out some forms, he headed toward the door. I followed and put my sunglasses over my eyes. He said, "I suppose those glasses do something fancy also." I said, "They do actually." As we stepped outside I showed him that if he looked closely, he could see the Ten Commandments on the lenses. A year or so earlier someone had sent the glasses to me as a gift. You could see the Commandments on the outside of the lenses, but you couldn't see them while you were wearing them. He was impressed. I quickly followed with, "Do you think you have kept the Ten Commandments—are you a good person?"

"Yes, I am."

"Have you ever lied?"

"Yes."

"What does that make you?"

"A liar."

"Have you ever stolen anything?"

"Yes."

"What does that make you?"

"A thief."

"Have you ever used God's name in vain?"

"Yes."

"That's called blasphemy, and it's a very serious crime in God's sight. Jesus said, 'Whoever looks upon a woman to lust after her has committed adultery already with her in his heart.' Have you ever looked at a woman with lust?"

"Yes, I have."

"Dennis, by your own admission, you are a lying, thieving adulterer at heart. If God were to judge you by the Ten Commandments on Judgment Day, do you think you would be innocent or guilty?"

"I'd be guilty."

"Would you go to Heaven or Hell?"

Dennis thought for about 15 seconds, and said, "I think that I will go to Heaven."

"The Bible says, 'All liars will have their part in the Lake of Fire.' No thief, adulterer, blasphemer, or fornicator will inherit the Kingdom of God."

He soberly said, "I would go to Hell then."

I could see that he was very concerned and said, "That should take your breath away with horror."

"What if I decided to change things from now on?"

I took him to civil law and said, "That's like a criminal expecting a judge to let him go because he said he wouldn't break the law anymore. The judge can't simply let him go. He's bound by law to punish him. What are you going to do?"

Dennis conceded, "You're right."

Each time he brought up something he could do to save himself, it was shot down in flames by taking his case back to civil law. Each time he would humbly say, "You're right."

After a few minutes I said, "If you died right now, you would go to Hell forever. What are you going to do?"

His mouth was stopped. He had run out of hope. I said, "Do you know what God did for you so that you wouldn't have to go to Hell?"

"Jesus Christ."

"That's right. He sent His Son to suffer for your sins. He paid your fine in His life's blood."

I labored the Cross for a moment and then asked if his family were Christians. He said that they were and how he felt pressured as a youth brought up in a Christian environment. But there was no more defensiveness. It was as though he was saying, "My family was right."

I asked if we could pray together, and we bowed our heads in the parking lot as I asked God to remind him of his secret sins, to give him understanding of the Cross, and to keep him and his family in health.

We then parted and I went to pick up my repaired van from just down the street. I remember thinking, "I wish I had a *What Hollywood Believes* book to give to Dennis."

As I sat in my van a few minutes later, I noticed one copy of *What Hollywood Believes* between the seats. I drove back to the rental place, walked into the lobby, and handed Dennis the book. He loudly said, "You wrote this book!" to a point where all the other workers came over to see what I had given him. Wide-eyed, he said, "My parents have this book at home."

23

My Enthusiastic Neighbor

by Ray Comfort

One of our neighbors looked a little scary. For months I would see him sitting outside of his little house on a cane chair, smoking a cigarette. He had long hair, a gray beard, and a missing front tooth. I did once witness to him and was surprised at his congeniality. That's the reason I began waving to him each day as I rode my bike past his house. I found that he didn't just acknowledge me; he would give an enthusiastic wave, sometimes with both hands. After riding by and waving dozens of times, I decided I would stop and try to talk to him about his salvation. He didn't exactly look the picture of health as he puffed on his cigarette, and I imagined one day the cane chair would be empty because death would snatch him into eternity.

It was around noon on a warm Sunday. I was on my bike and when I saw him, I rode onto his lawn right up to his chair, and asked, "Don't you get bored, sitting here every day?"

"Nope. My wife left me six months ago."

"She did?"

"Yep. Took everything. Everything. Nope, I don't get bored. I look forward to the next day. I'm moving soon to Yucca Valley. I have relatives up there. After I have been to the hospital ..."

"Hospital? Are you okay?"

"Just a check up. I'm a veteran. Only costs two dollars a visit."

Then he talked in detail about his days in the Army. I let him talk uninterrupted for about five minutes.

"Last time I spoke with you, we talked about the things of God. Have you given it any more thought?"

"Huh?"

"What do you think happens after someone dies?"

"Nobody knows. When I die, I'll just go into the ground and that's it."

"I thought you said, 'Nobody knows.'"

"Huh?"

"There is one way to know where you are going. Have you ever told a lie?"

"Yes."

"What does that make you?"

"A liar."

"Have you ever stolen anything?"

"When I was a kid. Candy."

"Have you ever used God's name in vain?"

"Plenty of times."

"Jesus said, 'Whoever looks at a woman to lust after her has committed adultery already with her in his heart.' Have you ever looked at a woman with lust?"

"Yes."

"By your own admission, you are a lying, thieving, blasphemous adulterer at heart. And you have to face God on Judgment Day. If God judges you by the Ten Commandments on that day, do you think that you will be innocent or guilty?"

"I would be guilty."

"Would you go to Heaven or Hell?"

"I don't believe in Hell."

"*If* God judges you by the Ten Commandments, the Bible says that you would end up in Hell. Doesn't that concern you?"

"It doesn't worry me at all."

"Would you sell one of your eyes for a million dollars?"
"Huh?"
"Would you sell one of your eyes for a million dollars?"
"I would sell this one. Can't see out of it."
"What about your other one?"
"No!"
"You value your eyes? How much more then is your soul worth? Of course, you don't want to go to Hell. I don't want you to go to Hell. Do you know what God did for you so that you wouldn't have to go to Hell?"
"He gave His only 'forgotten' Son?"
"Jesus took the punishment for your sins. Do you have a Bible?"
"The wife took it. Took everything. I can't even afford beer. I haven't had a beer for twenty-seven days."
"How about food?"
"No. Not much in the house."
"Can I make you lunch?"
"Huh? Sure."
"Do you like chicken?"
"Yes."
"Lettuce?"
"Nope. The wife choked on some. Almost died. Since then I'm scared to eat lettuce."
"Tomatoes?"
"Yep. I love tomatoes!"
"What's your name again?"
"Alan."
"Okay, Alan. I'll be back in ten minutes."

I rushed home, heated some chicken, sliced a tomato and a piece of watermelon, and grabbed some cheese and an *Evidence Bible*.

As I walked toward Alan, his good eye almost popped out of his head as he stared at the colorful platter.

He then balanced the plate on his knees, took hold of *The Evidence Bible*, shook my hand, and asked, "What's your name?"

"Ray."

"Huh?"

"Ray."

"Rah?"

"No, Ray."

"Okay. Ray."

As I left, Alan called out "You're the man. Thank you!"

That made me feel real good. A little good work speaks louder to a hungry man than a lot of good words.

24

Jesus Uncensored

by Ray Comfort

A Baptist Press report is suggesting that one of the reasons Southern Baptists are facing struggles with their evangelism efforts is that many church members may not be saved themselves. Tom Rainer, the dean of the Billy Graham School of Missions, in a recent study found that the evangelistic effectiveness of the denomination has remained fairly stagnant since 1950. The study's assessment is that nearly one-half of all church members (eleven million) may not be Christians.[4] He suggested that if these professing believers didn't care about the lost, they are not even saved.

The Southern Baptists aren't stagnating alone. Statistics show that 98 percent of the Church in the United States is in the same state. In the light of that thought, look at these alarming words of Jesus:

> *"If anyone is ashamed of me and my words in this adulterous and sinful generation, the Son of Man will be ashamed of him when he comes in his Father's glory with the holy angels" (Mark 8:38).*

Look at what Jesus said: "Whoever is ashamed of me *and of my words.*" Most of us are not ashamed of *Jesus.* In fact, studies have shown that as many as 62 percent of Americans say that they have a relationship with Jesus Christ that is "meaningful to them." There's no real problem with Jesus. It's the second part of that verse that's alarming. It's the *words* of Jesus we struggle with. Paul addressed this when he wrote to Timothy:

"For God has not given us the spirit of fear; but of power, and of love, and of a sound mind. Be not therefore ashamed of the testimony of our Lord ... but be a partaker of the afflictions of the gospel according to the power of God" (2 Timothy 1:8).

He said that Timothy wasn't to be ashamed *of the testimony of our Lord.* What was the "testimony of our Lord"? What did Jesus *testify*? He tells us in John 7:7: "The world cannot hate you; but me it hates, *because I testify of it*, that the works thereof are evil" (italics added). If you study the Scriptures, you will see that Jesus didn't have a problem with persecution until He opened His gracious mouth and testified. *And neither will you and I.* We won't have any problem with the "afflictions of the gospel" if we simply worship God, read our Bibles, and stagnate in church, listening to sermons.

But Jesus didn't stagnate in a pew. He *testified* as a True and Faithful witness. He "preached righteousness in the great congregation," and that's why they hated Him. He straightened the Law that the Pharisees had twisted. He opened up its divine precepts. He preached the fear of the Lord, and spoke openly of sin, righteousness, and judgment. He warned of a literal Hell and everlasting damnation, saying that God would hold us accountable for even every idle word. Not one "jot" or "tittle" of the Law that they had set aside would fail.

So Jesus warned that whoever was "ashamed" of Him *and His words,* of him He would be ashamed before the Father and the angels. *Vine's Expository Dictionary* says the word "ashamed" comes from a Greek word *aischos*, which means "to have a feeling of fear or shame which prevents a person from doing a thing." Doesn't that pinpoint our problem? If you and I "have a feeling of fear or shame" that prevents us from sharing our faith, then we are ashamed of Jesus and His words. We are ashamed when we should be saying what Paul said to Timothy:

"For the which cause I also suffer these things: nevertheless I am not ashamed: *for I know whom I have believed, and am persuaded that he is able to keep that which I have committed unto him against that day"* *(2 Timothy 1:12).*

Paul gives the solution to the problem of being ashamed to Timothy in the next chapter. He said, "Study to show yourself approved to God, a workman that *needs not to be ashamed…"* (2 Timothy 2:15).

You and I *need not* be ashamed. In other words, the problem has a solution. He said, *"Study* to show yourself approved to God." *Study* how to share your faith. It's as simple as that. Study the subject. A great preacher once said, "It is the great business of every Christian to save souls. People complain that they do not know how to take hold of this matter. Why, the reason is plain enough; *they have never studied it.* They have never taken the proper plans to qualify themselves for the work. *If you do not make it a matter of study,* how you may successfully act in building up the kingdom of Christ, you are acting a very wicked and absurd part as a Christian."

Let's then briefly study how to reach the lost. Let's look to Paul doing this, in Romans 2:21-24:

"You, then, who teach others, do you not teach yourself? You who preach against stealing, do you steal? You who say that people should not commit adultery, do you *commit adultery? You who abhor idols, do* you *rob temples? You who brag about the law, do you*

dishonor God by breaking the law? As it is written: 'God's name is blasphemed among the Gentiles because of you'" (emphases added).

So there's *how* to do it. Simply learn how to go through the Ten Commandments and personalize them with the person to whom you are speaking. Do you think you could do that? I think you could, *if you are so inclined.*

Are You Ready to Order?

Have you ever seen an eagle's nest? It's way up there—a thousand feet up on the edge of a cliff, and the mother eagle is saying to her poor chick, "Get out and fly." He's terrified, and that's understandable because he's never done that before. He prefers the cozy comfort and safety of his mother's nest. So, she takes all the feathers from the lining of the nest, leaving bare sticks to prod the eaglet, making it uncomfortable for him. Now he prefers to get out of the nest and stretch his wings.

Think of that little eaglet. He's never seen himself in a mirror. He doesn't know that God has given him wings. He has unseen muscles and perfectly positioned feathers. God has given him the ability to fly. All he has to do is take a step of faith off the high cliff to experience the purpose for which God has created him. But he will never experience flight until he takes that step.

I hope that what Jesus said about being ashamed of us (if we are ashamed of Him and His words) has removed some feathers from your nest. I hope your conscience is prodding you to move out of a cozy state of stagnation. If you are genuinely saved, God has given you everything you need to carry out His will. You have your wings. But you will never know that until you step out in faith. Take courage. Take that first step.

The Ugly Bullfrog

Jesus said, "You have not chosen me, but I have chosen you, and ordained you, that you should go and bring forth fruit, and that your fruit should remain" (John 15:16). Compare that to a parable Jesus told in Luke 13, just after He spoke of the necessity to repent. He said, "A man had a fig tree planted in his vineyard, and he went to look for fruit on it, but did not find any. So he said to the man who took care of the vineyard, 'For three years now I've been coming to look for fruit on this fig tree and haven't found any. Cut it down! Why should it use up the soil?' 'Sir,' the man replied, 'leave it alone for one more year, and I'll dig around it and fertilize it. If it bears fruit next year, fine! If not, then cut it down.'"

When the fig tree was fruitless, the owner said, "Cut it down! Why should it use up the soil?" I know how he felt. In spring of 2005 I built a greenhouse and planted twenty-two tomato plants, using three different varieties. For two months I watched over them with tender loving care. I watered them regularly, sprayed them, prayed over them, and even talked nicely to them.

Then I did a careful inspection of all twenty-two plants. They were huge—over six feet tall. Do you know how many tomatoes were on them? Four! Two were the size of my thumbnail, and they had been that size for more than a month. One was the size of my big toe, and the fourth professing tomato was so ugly, I didn't want to go near it. It looked like a bullfrog with warts.

As I was looking for fruit, I picked up a hard plastic label from the ground and read it. It showed a picture of a huge red tomato and said, "Produces high yields of tasty fruit all summer. Great for slicing." I wasn't impressed at how big the plants had become. I wanted to see the expected fruit. So I can understand why the owner in Luke 13 indignantly said, "Cut it down! Why should it use up the soil?" But the man who took care of the vineyard said, " ... leave it alone for one more year, and I'll dig around it and fertilize it. If it bears fruit next year, fine! If not, then cut it down."

It is my hope that if you haven't a deep concern for the lost, your conscience is sensitive to the digging around and fertilizing of the Holy Spirit. Is God speaking to you right now about your complacency?

The Odd One

I have often looked at Revelation 21:8 and thought that there seemed to be an odd one in the list of those who will be cast into the Lake of Fire. Look at what is says:

> "*The fearful, and unbelieving, and abominable, and murderers, and fornicators, and sorcerers, and idolaters, and all liars, shall have their part in the lake which burns with fire and brimstone: which is the second death.*"

Why are the "fearful" aligned with the unbelieving, the abominable, murderers, fornicators, sorcerers, idolaters, and liars? All these are obvious sins. Is being "fearful" therefore a "sin"? The word used in Scripture for "fearful" is the Greek word *deilos.* It's also used in Matthew 8:26 when the disciples became fearful during a storm. Jesus said, "Why are you fearful, O you of little faith?" When we are fearful in this respect, we lack faith in God. The Bible says, "God has not given us the spirit of fear, but of power, love and a sound mind." *Vine's Expository Dictionary* says it's the same Greek word *deilos* and comments that the word "… is never used in a good sense." God has not given us the spirit of fear, but He has instead given us one of power to witness, love to cast out all fear, and a sound mind to reason with the lost.

So, again, dear Christian, God has fully equipped you for flight. You have your wings. So don't be fearful. Take that step of faith. Make today a day of decision to fly with the message of the gospel, and together we will mount up with wings as eagles, and reach this world for Jesus Christ.

25

Old MacCameron
Had a Farm

by Kirk Cameron

I've always wanted a chicken. I love farm animals of all kinds, but there is something about those fuzzy little birds that I am particularly fond of. Luke, my four-year-old son, recently hatched some chicks in his preschool classroom and I practically trampled some toddlers on my way to the brooder to see them. I was jealous of those kids for having chickens, and I finally broke down—determined to get my own. But I couldn't just go to the store and buy them, because I am a married man. Married men don't do such selfish things without first consulting with their wives.

So I devised a plan to convince Chelsea to welcome these fowl creatures into our family. Here's what I did. One morning, I suggested that Chelsea get away for a few hours and relax while I watched the kids. While she was gone, I took my three youngest children on a field trip to the local farm animal feed store, where I knew they sold the cutest baby chicks in town, and let my two-, three-, and four-year-old children each select and hold their favorite chicks, name them, and carry them in their arms for an hour. As we left the store, my babies had tears in their eyes, not wanting to leave the baby chicks behind. I then asked the kids, "If you were to have chicks of your own, do you think you could take very good care of them?"

"Yes, yes!" they replied. "Oh, please, Daddy! Can we please get some baby chicks?"

"We'll, it's okay with me, but you'll have to ask your mother," I replied, as any responsible husband would. "But if you really want a chick," I said, "you'll have to tell your mommy how much you truly love chicks and promise to take good care of them every day. Would you kids like to tell your mommy that?" I asked.

"Oh, yes, Daddy! We'll tell her as soon as we get home! Thank you, Daddy! Thank you!" my little girl Olivia exclaimed.

The deal was done! There was no turning back. How could my wife possibly resist the plea of her own precious little daughter? I could practically smell the fresh eggs. In my mind, I had already become a chicken farmer.

My plan to secure some chickens at home worked like a charm. Two weeks later my sons and I were building a chicken coop in the backyard, complete with rafters to perch on, nests to lay eggs in, and hay to scratch on. We purchased the chicks (one for each of our six children) and let the kids name them: Angel, Gloria, Jasmine, Blackie, James, and Cutie Pie.[5]

Having chickens has taught me a few things about God. I've learned that none of us is a natural born follower of Christ. Each of us had to come out of our shell, mount up with wings as eagles, and lay aside our lives for the sake of the gospel. We had to learn not to "flock together" with our sinful, worldly-minded friends as we did before we came to Christ, and instead be set apart, transformed by the renewing of our minds. Becoming a Christian has put us low on the world's pecking order, but we know that God has "chosen the foolish things of the world to confound the wise; and ... the weak things ... to confound the things which are mighty; and ... the base things ... and things which are despised ... and things which are not, to bring to nothing things that are" (1 Corinthians 1:27, 28). It's good to be a lowly creature, because as lowly Christians, we are "more than conquerors through Him who loved us" (Romans 8:37).

Three months later, the chickens are now full-grown and not so cute. They make more messes than my six kids combined and they still don't lay eggs. I regularly make chicken soup for dinner in hopes that the steaming aroma will drift across the chicken coop in the backyard, reminding those freeloading feathered friends to lay some eggs soon … or else.

I still love chickens! They're fun to watch and good to eat. But more than that, they are a daily reminder to me of the lowly creature that I am, and how cowardly I would act without the power of Christ to help me live as I ought.

26

Ten Out of Ten

by Ray Comfort

Larry Lee is another good friend of our ministry. He often shares his witnessing adventures with us, so we thought that you might be interested to see how he relates to the unsaved. The following are three of his witnessing encounters:

Yesterday, we had an open house from 2-5 p.m., trying to get some additional traffic in to see our home.

So we had to get lost for those three hours while our real estate agent worked the crowd. We went to an amusement park with the kids.

I was not excited about going to the park—my mind was on selling the house, and I just don't enjoy thinking about the fact that people are snooping around my house when I'm not there.

So I went to the park with my family, dragging my feet, feeling sorry for myself. Plus, I don't go on any rides. I'm not a ride person. I prefer throwing the baseball that clocks your speed and shooting hoops to win prizes—but this place was rides only. Bummer.

So Ashley[6] and the kids hit the rides, and I'm standing there watching. I noticed that the people running the rides were all in their late teens or early 20s. They just stand there during the rides, looking totally bored. So I walked up to the guy running the ride that my family was on and this kid was wearing a WWJD bracelet. I said, "Hey man, cool bracelet."

He smiled and said, "Thanks."

I asked, "Have you had a Christian background?"

He said, "Oh, yes."

"Have you ever taken the Good Person Test?"

He looked at me and smiled, "No."

I said, "Are you ready?"

He said, "Sure."

Turns out he's a liar and an adulterer, and is disobedient to his parents. He said he never ever stole anything, so I gave him that one. He said he'd be guilty on Judgment Day, and when I asked Heaven or Hell, he said, "Hell."

I said, "Hell?"

And he shook his head yes. Here he is, telling me he has a Christian background, he's wearing a WWJD bracelet, and he's telling me he's going to Hell and he's worried. So I gave him the gospel and challenged him to make peace with God, and I left him with a *Left Behind II* tract.

We went to the next ride, and a girl was there, supervising another employee—so I chatted with her, gave her a million bucks, and told her it had a Christian message on the back.

She said, "Oh, okay … cool."

I asked, "Have you had a Christian background?"

"No," she said.

"Do you go to church?"

"No."

"Do you have a Bible?"

"No." Unreal. So I asked, "Have you ever taken the Good Person Test?"

She looked at me, smiled, and said, "No."

I asked, "Are you ready?"

She turned to me with genuine excitement and said, "Okay, let's do it."

She was a liar, a thief, an adulterer and a blasphemer. She said she'd be guilty and end up in Hell. Man, two people in a row, admitting that their destiny was Hell and they were concerned about it. I explained the gospel to her and challenged her to make things right with God before her head hit the pillow. I told her to visit the website on the *Left Behind II* tract and to write to the Web master and ask for a Bible and they'd charge it to me. She said, "Okay."

Guys, when she walked away, she said the sweetest, "Thank you," nodding her head and smiling. She was very, very thankful. It was amazing.

On to the next ride. And the next. And the next. These next three people, all the same thing—all guilty, all admitted they were headed for Hell. All admitted they needed to make things right with God. I gave them all millions and *Left Behind II* tracts. Then I talked to Cody, a kid working the snack bar. He was just standing there with no customers, so I became his next customer—incredible talk.

As soon as he said, "Hell," his boss walks in. Cody is staring at me like, "Dude, don't go now, I'm headed for Hell, what should I do?" I small-talked with the boss, telling him how Cody was the coolest employee and deserved a big raise and a company car. He laughed and then finally left. I got to tell Cody the good news. Cody said he had a Baptist background, but he hadn't been to church since he was six years old. He was now seventeen. Amazing!

Then I saw these two guys, Jerell and Lorenzo, putting out pine straw and sweeping the place. Again, got to go one-on-one with each of them individually. Both were headed for Hell; both said they needed to get right.

Then we went to the teacup ride, that dreadful ride where the world won't stop whirling around. Ashley had given the guy running the ride a million bucks, so I asked him if he had read the back. He had. I said, "Well, did you answer the million dollar question?"

He said, "Yeah, I'm not so sure."

I looked at his nametag. Guess what his name was? Jesus! But he was from Mexico, so of course he said it like, "Heysoose." I said, "I like that name a lot." He smiled. I asked him if he had a Christian background. He said he's Catholic, studying to get confirmed.

I said, "So have you ever taken the Good Person Test?"

He said, "No."

I said, "Are you ready?"

He smiled and said, "Yeah, let's hear it."

He was a liar, a thief, an adulterer, and a blasphemer. Guilty, going to Hell, and concerned. I told him how to make peace with God and left him with tracts.

Finally I talked with Jared, who was emptying all the trash cans around the park. You could tell this guy hated his job and was probably hoping that no one would notice him. So I gave him a big tip and told him I knew he was working hard and that the park looked really good from all his efforts.

He said, "Thanks."

I told him the Million Dollar Bill had a Christian message and then asked, "Have you had a Christian background?"

"Yes."

"So have you ever taken the Good Person Test?"

He looked at me sideways and said, "Not yet.

I asked, "Are you ready?"

He said, "Yeah, okay." Liar, thief, adulterer, etc. He said he'd be guilty.

I asked, "Heaven or Hell?" And he said, "Well, I'm really trying."

I said, "Jared, you've got to be perfect to get in, sinless."

He looked down and shook his head, and then I said, "So it sounds to me like Hell?" He shook his head, 'Yes.' He was crushed. Suddenly, I heard those three words that I really don't like to hear coming from behind me: "Excuse me, sir."

I thought, "Uh ohhhhh, busted." I turned and saw two middle-aged white guys, one wearing official park security garb and the other guy wearing regular clothes.

The security guy goes, "Sir, we know what you're doing."

I said, "Really? Great."

He said, "And you've got a good message; we appreciate your message, but we just can't have you talking to the employees."

The plainclothes guy said, "I'm an undercover private investigator and we've got to be careful in this place, and we just can't have you distracting the employees. If something happens to the kids on the rides and you are distracting them, we're all in for big trouble."

I said, "I certainly didn't mean to distract them. We just chatted as they were doing their work, but I understand what you're saying. I'd hate to see someone get hurt. I won't talk to them."

They said, "We appreciate it."

I said, "You know, I come to these parks and I'm too much of a wimp for these rides, but my kids love them. I'm just hanging around, totally bored and waiting for them, so I just enjoy striking up conversations."

The main dude said, "Well, you can talk to other people, just not the employees. We've had several people also complain about the message on the back of the Million Dollar Bills." (I'm thinking, "Perfect! The conscience is alive and well!") "We like your message, but you just need to avoid talking with employees."

I told them who I was, we shook hands, and they walked off. Suddenly I remembered Jared, the kid collecting trash. I had left the poor guy hanging over the brink of Hell, and now he was gone!

I looked around and saw him way down by some other rides. I thought, "I've got to at least give him another tract."

So I walked up to him and simply said, "Jared, I'm not allowed to talk to you anymore."

You should have seen his reaction. He looked down and shook his head at the same time, disgusted, like 'Man, what a joke.' I said, "But I want you to have this. Please read it carefully. God bless you." It was the *Left Behind II* tract. And I walked away.

I was a bit bummed, but then realized that in the past hour, I had spoken with ten people individually, and every single one of them admitted they were headed for Hell. Ten out of ten! That's huge! And now they all had tracts, and they all knew what they needed to do.

And strangely enough, I was no longer feeling sorry for myself that I had to go to the amusement park during the open house. I was thankful and went home, clicking my heels.

Fishing Story
In preparation for moving to Charlotte, we needed to have much of the inside of our house painted. The painting crew arrived on Tuesday, and they were in our house all week. This is the same crew that painted the outside of our house last fall. Ashley brought one of the guys on the crew through the Law and then gave him the gospel last fall, and he was born again later that night. Two days later, she brought the guy's son, who was also on the painting crew, through the Law and then gave him the gospel — he too accepted the Lord.

Now the owner of the company is a young, kind of tough-guy type, who really likes to wheel and deal. I don't like the wheel and deal approach, so we pretty much butted heads from the start. You know, one of those guys where you walk away saying, "I'm not gonna witness to that guy—he's a jerk, he'll never accept this." Sure, Larry.

His name is John. So all week the crew is here at the house — it was crazy. But John did not return until late yesterday to look over everything and collect the money. In the meantime, however, another guy came to our house this week—this guy's name was Johnny. Johnny gave us a quote on replacing our kitchen counter, and then quickly left. Ashley handed him a Giant Money on the way out, and I followed him out to his truck. This guy was 55 years old, kind of a quiet guy, and I said, "Hey, Johnny, that money has a great Christian message on the back—have you had a Christian background?"

He opened up the passenger door of his truck and said quietly, "No, not really."

I said, "Well, what do you think is on the other side when people die? What's your opinion?"

He stared off into space and said, "I don't know."

I said, "Do you ever think about stuff like this?"

He said, "No."

So I asked, "Johnny, would you consider yourself to be a good person?"

Now get this—he goes, "Yes!" As quick as lightning, jumps in the *passenger side of the car*, slams the door, jumps over to the driver's seat, starts the engine, and takes off! Johnny ran away from me! I've never had someone actually run away from me—I just stood there like a total doofus in my front yard, staring at the dust flying up behind Johnny's truck as he sped away. Boy, did I feel cool.

So the next day, tough guy John arrives on the scene. Of course, I'm thinking he's gonna totally blow me off. He didn't—he listened, he squirmed under the Law, was relieved by Grace, and said he was going to give this some serious thought. I gave him a copy of *What Hollywood Believes*.

But here's where yet another John comes in—as I'm witnessing to tough-guy John in my driveway, my neighbor across the street whose name is, you guessed it, *John*, who thinks I'm wacko, comes out into the street and turns on his leaf blower—the loudest leaf blower in existence, mind you. He's just standing there at the end of his driveway, blowing some miscellaneous leaves around. He started this right as I was going through the Law, and explaining the courtroom scene. Nice timing.

Thankfully, the leaf blower finally went off, and tough guy John, who wasn't so tough after all, took the book … and all was well.

Mike, the AAA Guy

This morning, I went to an 8:00 a.m. meeting at Starbucks. On my way there, I was asking God to please use me to share the truth with someone.

I arrived at Starbucks about six minutes late, and I was talking with my wife on the cell phone. We finished our conversation; I got out of the car, locked and shut the door, and took off toward the Starbucks' entrance. Suddenly I had this awful feeling that I had left my keys in the car. I quickly checked all my pockets—no keys. I ran back to the car and looked on the front seat—keys. I thought, "Doofus! You did it again!" I took off for Starbucks again, wondering how I was going to have a productive meeting when I knew I would be kicking myself during the entire meeting about locking the keys in the car.

Well, we had a good meeting. After the meeting, I called AAA and requested someone to come and unlock the car. It took an hour and a half for the guy to show up. It was cold and windy outside. While I waited, I decided to get my hair cut at Sport Clips next to Starbucks—so at least I had that going for me. I gave the women who worked there Million Dollar Bill tracts and Curved Illusion: pink and blue tracts. Then I went to do some quick Christmas shopping for my parents at Golf Galaxy. I gave the guy there a million bucks, too.

Then I went and got some more coffee and gave out some more tracts.

Then Mike showed up. Mike was a really cool guy in his 30s or early 40s who drove the tow truck for AAA. He tried for about 45 minutes to jimmy my car door open, but to no avail. It was really cold outside ... and windy. He was not having fun and neither was I. I was actually feeling quite sorry for myself, because I had "so much to do" today.

Then I smacked myself upside the head—duh, witness to the guy. Mike had just mentioned that he used to work in a hospital and now he was doing this tow-truck thing. I told him that I used to work in financial planning, and now I was running a Christian ministry.

He said, "Christian ministry? What kind of Christian ministry?"

"Well, I teach Christians how to reach out with the gospel and how to answer questions that come up during conversations"—like I'm about to do with you, buddy.

Huh?"

"Have you had a Christian background?"

"Yeah, you know, I went to church growing up and all that. I guess you could say I was a middle class kid and we went to church and all, but you know, I was just thinking about this stuff this morning."

"What stuff?"

"You know, like getting God into my life. You know, I really want to give my life to God, but I just don't know how to do that."

TIME OUT: I am not kidding, this is exactly what the guy said. I would not make this up.

"Mike, you know what will really help bring it all together for you?"

"What's that?"

"Looking at the Ten Commandments."

"Really?"

"Yup, that's exactly what you need to do, because it will clarify for you exactly where you stand with God, and it will help you see how the gospel really makes sense. Can I ask you a couple of questions?"

"Shoot."

"Have you ever lied?"

"Oh, yeah."

"What does that make you?"

"A sinner."

"But more specifically, what does it make you?"

He looked right at me and paused, and then he said, "A liar." It was so interesting. Up to this point, he had been looking away, then glancing at me, and then looking away. Even when he said, "A sinner," he was looking this way and that. But when he said, "A liar," he just stared at me.

"How about stealing? Did you ever steal something when you were younger?"

"Yeah."

"So what does that make you?"

Before I finished that question, he said, "Yeah, a thief."

"Jesus said that looking with lust is the same as adultery in God's eyes—have you ever done that?"

"Yes."

"How about using God's name in vain?"

Down went the eyes. He nodded his head and said, "Yeah."

"Do you see the problem here, Mike? This is like looking into a mirror—you are seeing yourself compared to God's perfect standard. We've only gone through four of the Commandments, and you told me that you are a liar, a thief, an adulterer, and a blasphemer."

"That's right."

"So if God judged you today, would you be innocent or guilty?"

"Guilty. Definitely!"

"So what do you think will be your destiny—Heaven or Hell."

He just shook his head. Then he said, "Hell."

"You don't want that, do you?"

"No."

"The Bible makes it clear that no one who is unrighteous can enter God's kingdom—no thief, or liar, or adulterer, or blasphemer. You don't want to end up there, Mike."

"I know."

"Do you see the problem you have?"

"Yeah."

"Here's the solution. God does not want you to go to Hell. He did not make Hell for you—He made it for Satan and his angels. But man rebelled and decided to go against God, so God demanded justice. See, God is loving, but He is also just. He will punish sin. He must, by His nature, punish sin."

Mike said, "But what I don't understand is why God had to die—why did Jesus have to die?"

"God demands justice," I said. "Perfect justice. And the price that must be paid for sin is death. Since God's justice is perfect, He demands a perfect sacrifice for sin. Jesus is that perfect sacrifice. He didn't lie, or steal, or commit adultery or do anything like that during His life. He lived a perfect life. Then He willingly sacrificed His life for us—to pay the fine for us. He gave His life so you wouldn't have to give yours. Do you know what that's called?"

"What?"

"Love."

He nodded his head.

"Love is not some sappy feeling of warm fuzzies that you get when you think about God. Love is action. It is doing to others, as you would have them do to you. It is sacrificing yourself for others, which is exactly what Jesus did for us. So the reason Jesus had to die was to satisfy God's perfect justice. And if you trust Jesus as Lord and Savior, you will not have to receive God's justice. And that's a good deal."

"Yeah."

I brought him through a courtroom scene, helping him see how someone paying a fine on the behalf of another person is truly a loving thing to do, a gift. And that gift is not given because we deserve it, but because we are loved by God. I told him that today he needed to surrender his life to Jesus Christ— that he needed to repent of his sins and put his faith in Jesus.

He then told me that he had done so much bad stuff that he couldn't really go to God at this point.

I told him, "If you're sick, you don't try to get yourself better before you go see the doctor. You go to the doctor in order to get better. You're telling me that you need to get cleaned up before you go to God, but only God can actually clean you— you can't clean yourself. That's like trying to jump over the Grand Canyon—you can't even get started."

"But I've been sinning a lot; my personal life stinks, man. I try to listen to Christian music. I try to pray, and things go okay for a while, and then bam, off I go again, sinning and doing bad stuff."

"You'll never get out of that rut until you surrender your life to Jesus Christ, Mike. The only way to have power to stop sinning is to have the Holy Spirit within you. And the only way to have the Holy Spirit within you is to be born again—to repent of your sins and put your faith in Jesus Christ. That's when you will begin to see that you can start living right. You won't be perfect; you can still mess up. But that does not mean you should try to mess up and say, 'Hey, I'm only human, I'm gonna mess up anyway.' No, you should try to honor God every day with your life, showing Him how much you love Him by obeying His word. See what I'm saying?"

"Yeah."

I went on to tell him that Jesus did not come to solve all of his problems, but He did come to solve Mike's biggest problem—sin, and the resulting Judgment and Hell. I told him how he could grow closer to God every day once he gets saved. I told him that he would need to make some tough decisions, but that the Holy Spirit would help him say no to the stuff that's wrong and yes to the stuff that's good. I told him that I wasn't sure if he lived with his girlfriend or not—he had mentioned his girlfriend when he talked about sinning, but that he would have to make the decision to stop having sex with her until they got married, and if she didn't like that, then she would need to hit the highway. He smiled and nodded.

Basically, I told him what Jesus told His hearers—that there is a cost to being a disciple. I was not trying to scare him away, but I wanted him to understand that the only way to Heaven was through Jesus, and that requires turning away from sin and towards God. I told him that God would never throw him out of Heaven if he slipped up and sinned. But I also told him that we should not go out and sin because we're 'good to go' with God.

He understood. He said, "I think God wanted me to talk to you today. I have been really struggling and wanting to get right with God, but I just wasn't sure how."

I said, "Now you know, right?"

"Yes."

"Mike, this is not between you and me; it's between you and God. But if I were you, I would get on my knees as soon as possible, call out to God, and surrender your life to him. Repent of your sins and put your trust in Jesus. And then dive into the Word daily. And call me if you want to come to a solid church."

"Yeah, I need a solid church. Can I have your card?"

So I gave him my card, some tracts, and we parted ways. But before he left, I asked if I could pray for him.

He said, "Sure."

So I extended my hand. We shook hands, and I just held onto his hand as we prayed. I thanked God for bringing Mike to help me out with my car and prayed that Mike would make the most important decision of his life—to trust in Jesus Christ. I prayed that Mike would then live out his life in gratitude to God every day. As I was praying, he kept increasing the pressure of his grip on my hand to the point where I was starting to realize that this guy was a lot stronger that I was! We finished up and parted ways.

He called me later to make sure that I got into the car all right. He could not get the car open for me and had to call for backup, so I got to give tracts to the next guy too. Mike also thanked me on the phone several times for talking to him. It was really cool.

By the way, I told him that once he made peace with God, the most amazing experience is sharing the truth of the gospel with people just like I had just done with him. He said, "Really?" with a big smile.

I said, "You bet. There's nothing like it. I'm telling you, it's the deal."

He said, "That's cool."

* * *

Here's another testimony. This one is from a man named Erik Myhrberg:

On a recent flight between California and Arizona I was given two opportunities to use your approach to biblical evangelism. On my outbound flight I was fortunate to have boarded the small plane first, and have gotten an aisle seat in row one. As I was reading a magazine, a woman boarded the plane heavily laden and carrying hot coffee, which she promptly spilled across my lap and continued boarding without realizing what she had done. My initial response was, "That's hot coffee in my lap and I haven't got a parachute on."[7]

I asked the male flight attendant for some napkins, and while people continued to board, he was becoming more irate about the woman's lack of attention while I was just sitting there smiling at the fact that I had just lived through one of Ray's analogies! As we prepared to land, I spoke to the flight attendant and handed him one of the Bible tracts (*101 One Liners*[8]), using humor about what had happened with the coffee to share the literature.

It was the return flight that I really would like to tell you about. I boarded early and was again sitting in the tiny aisle seat in the first row. The flight was pretty full and the seat next to me remained open. As the last passenger boarded, she looked at her boarding card and said, "I'm in the seat next to you."

I thought "Great. Now I have no place to set my book down." I am reading *The Way of the Master*[9], and was heavily engrossed in Chapter 16, "How to Share Your Faith," when the realization hit me that I am supposed to do what the book recommends on an ongoing basis.

I am not a shy person, and I do a great deal of public speaking as part of my consultancy. But when issues of such great importance as eternal life come up, I get very still. As I sat in my seat I realized that this person next to me might not be safe from the judgment to come. That bothered me. I closed the book and asked God to give me the courage to speak up for Him. I looked over and saw that she was reading a book. It was open and as I scanned the page facing me the word "God" was what I read first. As I thought what that might mean, she looked up at me. I smiled and asked, "Good book?" She immediately turned toward me and told me that it was, but that she had only just started it.

"What is it about?" I asked. She explained it was a fictional story about a man who writes obituaries for a newspaper.

Without thinking I asked "What do you think will happen when you die?"

She looked very closely at me and said "That could take hours to answer and debate."

From there, I stuck to the WDJD[10] that my wife and I have been studying these past few weeks. I walked her through the "Would you consider yourself to be a good person?" right into several of the Ten Commandments, and then straight to

Judgment Day. Her name was Tracy and she listened very carefully, asked questions, and slowly dropped her head as we spoke.

This occurred over a fifteen-minute period from final approach to parking at the gate. She was going to a wedding, and wanted to share what she had just heard with her husband. Additionally, her mother-in-law and friend had been trying to get her into a Bible study for some time, but had never explained "it" this way. I handed her a Bible tract (for Web site reference) and gave her a shiny new penny with the Ten Commandments on it.[11] I asked her to really consider what we had talked about and to read her Bible when she got home.

Fifteen minutes earlier, I had sat in my tiny seat with hot sweat running down my back, and now I was skipping through the terminal and down to my wife. Part of our graduation requirements is to share the WDJD with others (including total strangers). What a great requirement to have in place!

* * *

The following account is from Joshua Williamson (Australia):

Tonight there was a big river festival in Brisbane City, so a few others and I went up to preach. I met up with a new seed-sower[12] contact in the city, and while we were talking he said he wanted to learn to preach "open-air," but had never seen it done "live." So I said, "That's all right because I am about to preach."

So I set up the little stool, jumped up, and started to speak. Within seconds, a large crowd of Satanist Goths assembled and sat down to listen to the gospel. This grew to a bigger crowd of between 200-300 or more. I went through the Law, and pronounced how sin has put the death sentence on humanity. Then all Hell literally broke loose. They started heckling, which was fine, as this grew the crowd, but then some Goth started throwing things at me from behind. This wasn't much—just annoying. But as it progressed, people started to punch me, but I preached on. Then some guy ran at me from behind and pushed me off the stool. Then all these Goths started to hit, kick, and spit on me.

So I jumped back up and kept preaching. Now they started throwing glass and plastic bottles at me. One hit me in the mouth, but still I had to keep preaching. It was like I could feel the power of God flowing around me, and I knew I had to keep going.

One little lesbian was the loudest. She was punching me and kicking all the time. Then someone lit a bit of paper and put it on me. So now my neck was on fire. It quickly went out with no pain. Then some guy put a lit cigarette down my shirt. Again no pain. They started kicking and throwing stuff again—I don't think they ever stopped. When some other Christians saw this, they came over to support in prayer, etc.

While they were still going on, I kept preaching repentance, which they hated. Then after about fifty minutes of preaching, I stopped. Yet they didn't want to. It was then that some Satanist stabbed me in the back with a pointy metal spike. Another Goth filled a bottle with something and lit it on fire, but as he went to throw it, the flames stopped, much to his surprise. Another Satanist threw a bottle at me, but another one stepped in the way and got hit in the back of the head. Two Goths started fighting each other—it was like the enemy was confused and fighting with himself. Then I got hit on the head with a metal can of something. That did hurt. The whole time, the police were watching, yet did nothing, even when a Christian went and spoke to them.

Slowly the crowd started to leave, and I was left standing there in pain with a few Christians praying. Then one "Christian" tried to tell me that the Spirit of God wasn't in my preaching, as no fruit was shown. It was then that two backslidden Christians, who were now Goths, came running up and informed me that they had repented and put their trust in God! You could see these two girls were on fire. They were praising God, and left all their Satanist friends. Also the few Christians there were excited about preaching the gospel. They said it set them on fire, and they want to learn how to share their faith, and come out to witness with us! GOD BE PRAISED!

At the end, a few Goths came up and thanked me for preaching, and even though they hated the message, they said they respected me for preaching. A lot of seed was sown, and the Kingdom of Heaven rejoices tonight!

The Way of the Master Testimonies:

"This is by far the best form of evangelism I have ever seen. In some ways I feel a bit foolish in that it has taken me so long to get it. I graduated Magma Cum Laude from Liberty Baptist Seminary in Apologetics. I had the best professors around (Norm Geisler, Gary Habermas, J.P. Moreland), and I have been gifted to debate with a cultist, religionist, atheist, etc. But now I see what was missing in my evangelism. All these years, I was communicating primarily to the intellect and not the conscience." – Pastor James Pannafino (New York).

* * *

Last night a small group of us went out to the Lenny Kravitz concert in Grand Prairie to pass out tracts. One of the first couples coming out was pretty drunk. When they each got a tract, they assured us that they were Christians and went to XYZ mega-church. They explained that they normally don't do that kind of thing, but it was their tenth anniversary and they "got a little carried away." They admitted to drinking too much.

Not a whole lot was said beyond the biblical gospel. In fact, the idea of true and false conversion wasn't even mentioned, but the husband began to come under conviction and said to his wife, "Lynne, I don't think we're true believers. We're not out here like these guys."

Lynne got upset with her husband and said, "What are you saying? Are you saying that we're not saved?"

"Lynne, if we were really saved, we would be out here like these guys! I don't know."

She finally got so upset that she stomped off in a huff. One of the others said that they saw her a little later and she looked very upset. The husband stayed a little longer and thanked God for us a few times for being out there. It was pretty wild. We had to laugh when he said two or three times that he thanked God for us. He admitted that it was not an accident that we ran into him, and was grateful. – Anonymous

* * *

Dear Brother Ray, I have been a pastor for 25 years. I always thought I was doing a reasonably good job. Kind of like the folks that tell you they consider themselves "good people." I had tried to preach what I thought was the whole counsel of God. I prayed over the years with many people to accept Jesus and make Him Lord of their lives.

My wife Judy and I moved to Ruidoso, New Mexico, about six years ago to plant a church. Shortly after arriving, I was convicted that something was horribly wrong with my ministry. I read the Scriptures and prayed earnestly that God would show me what was wrong. The feeling continued to grow and I became depressed and moody. I asked Judy to pray for me and explained my problem. I didn't know if this was the Holy Spirit convicting or Satan attacking. She prayed that God would reveal the cause of my depression and make Himself clear as He revealed any problem with my ministry for Him.

That night I had the most terrifying, realistic, blood-chilling nightmare any man has ever had. I am a Vietnam veteran and I know a little about nightmares. Nothing in my experience has ever come close to the horror of that night, nor do I ever want it to!

I dreamed that it was Judgment Day and I was standing right next to the Throne of God. I noticed that to my left and my right were pastors as far as I could see. I thought this was odd that the Lord would reserve this front row space for pastors only.

I looked out across a space of only a few yards and there were millions, maybe billions of people, yet I could see each one of their eyes staring at me. As I studied this group, I noticed that I knew many of them from times at the altar or ones who had sat under my teaching. I was pleased to see that they had made it to Heaven, but confused because they didn't look happy. They looked very angry and hateful.

Then I heard the voice of the Lord say, "Away, I never knew you."

I was suddenly frightened that what I was seeing were those who "thought" that they were saved. Then I saw all of them pointing a finger at each of us pastors and saying together in one voice that shook my soul, *"We sat in your church and thought we were saved. Why didn't you tell us we were lost?"*

Tears were pouring down my face and the faces of all of those pastors. I watched as one-by-one, those people were cast into Hell. One and then another, and another, and another—until they were all gone. I died inside as each one screamed in agony and gnashed their teeth, cursing us as they went into the Lake of Fire.

Then I was looking into the face of Jesus and He said to me, "Is this the part where I'm suppose to say, 'Well done, my good and faithful servant?'" I woke up with a scream and my heart pounding, and I was begging Jesus to forgive me.

I died a million deaths that night. Since that night I have done two things on a daily basis. I do everything I can to preach the Law before Grace in the hope that conviction of sin will bring a sinner to true salvation. The other thing that I do is pray for every person I have ever preached to, asking God to repair any damage I have done. I also never believe anyone when they tell me they are saved. It is my duty to challenge them and search out the solidness of their salvation.

Your ministry and material have been great blessings to me. I am learning to be more effective and confident as I teach others how to share their faith by using the Law. I have seen several people saved who thought they were saved, as I have used "The Way of the Master" material to teach them evangelism.

I do want to hear those words, "Well done, my good and faithful servant," and thanks to you and your team, I have a better chance of hearing them. Thank you! I just wanted to let you know that some pastors are waking up to the truth. The desire of my heart is to please God. I pray that my days of being a man-pleaser are over, along with the nightmares. I also pray that God will use me to bring other pastors into the truth of the gospel message so that they will not have to face the nightmare that I did. Blessings. – Steve Kreins, First Church of God, Waco, Texas

* * *

We have been studying "Hell's Best Kept Secret" at our church and I kept hearing people say, "normal people couldn't do that like Ray and Kirk do." So another member and I decided to make our own The Way of the Master video and show the church that truly anyone could walk up to a stranger and witness using this. We went to Indiana University and just began to walk the campus and talk to people. It was so easy and a very wonderful experience. In about a two-hour period we were able to witness to a Muslim, a Buddhist, two Jewish girls who claimed that Jews did not believe in the Ten Commandments, a Mormon student, and two atheists. We were just so encouraged that we were able share our faith with these people. I have now begun to use many of your tracts at my workplace to witness to my coworkers. I work in an underground coal mine, and let me just say that it isn't the best environment to witness to people in, but your tracts have made it extremely easy to do. Thank you for being so faithful and for teaching me how to truly witness to someone without just inviting them to go to church with me. – Craig H., Linton, Indiana

* * *

More Adventures
A good friend of ours named Joey Nicolosi is actually sponsored by his church to do nothing but evangelism for twenty hours a week. He keeps a journal on a Web site that he has called www.AdventuresinChristianity.com, where you can read more. Here are some of his adventures:

A coffee-house-style gathering was taking place at my college earlier this week. Each Thursday, a different performer comes, like a comedian, musician, etc. Well, I noticed that this week was "open-mic" night. Last year, I wanted to "open-mic" preach, but didn't have the courage to do it. This time, I decided to go for it. When the last performer ended his song, which was full of profanity, I got up and asked if anyone had a college ID card. I took one from an audience member and spun it around in the air, around my body and between my hands, using a magic trick. The crowd thought it was cool, and I had their full attention.

I brought up how this was only an illusion, yet there is another illusion many of us hold: the idea that we are basically good people. I laid out what I think was the most thorough gospel presentation I've ever done, carefully aiming the Ten Commandments at their consciences and pleading with them to think about their eternities, while reasoning with them out of deep concern that there can be no other way to escape Hell.

By the time I finished, the whole room looked stunned. No one moved. Students seemed shocked that a fellow peer would present something like this. As I finished, I thanked them for their time and open-mindedness, and headed back off the stage. After a moment or two of silence, quite a few students began to file silently outside, looking solemn.

After a bit, the performer before me got back up on stage with his guitar, and talked a little about how religion was "forced down his throat" when he was younger, and how he was sick of hearing the same Christian message over and over. I strongly doubt he ever heard the Commandments used that way, especially from a pleading fellow student, and *especially* not on our campus. After affirming that he too was a Christian, he then went back to singing his lighthearted and profane songs, but the ambiance just wasn't the same. The bullet had hit its mark.

What a night! I brought a friend named Sam out to the Calabasas Commons. Sam has never really gone out and used the Law, so she was skeptical and curious to see it done. The first few groups of young guys we spoke with were self-righteous and sure they deserve to go to Heaven, despite their sin. They said they weren't concerned at all about their eternal destiny.

One young guy I spoke with named Muhammad said he wasn't concerned about his eternal salvation, then said he was, and continued to go back and forth. I could see he wasn't serious, yet his avoidance of what I was saying (he seemed to be looking for distractions) showed me that something was going on.

Finally Nathan, who is a bit stronger and more blunt in his way with people, told this guy that the reason he was avoiding this issue was that he didn't want his deeds done in darkness to come to light. The guy continued to look away, and we left him and his friends with tracts, not speaking to him about Grace, since he didn't seem humbled by the Law.

Later, I saw Nicole and Carrie, two girls with whom we spoke last Friday night. I spoke with Carrie for a bit, and asked her if she had thought about our conversation from last week. I often wonder what happens with people *after* a witnessing conversation. She told me she and her friends went back home and read through the tracts together, and also squashed a fly with one of them.

"Oh, is this the guy you were talking about last week?" Carrie's friend asked.

"Uh-oh, what did she say?" I responded, half-joking.

"No, she mentioned how she had a really intelligent conversation with you last week, and that it was good."

After our conversation, I felt refueled. Meeting people like that gave me enough encouragement to go and witness for the rest of the night. Just knowing that this girl really took in what we were talking about and what it meant to her makes all this worth it.

Sam and I decided to talk to one more group of people before going home. I spotted two girls talking by one of the fountains. I interrupted their conversation at a lull, and gave them the "Good Person" tracts, asking if they wanted to take the Good Person Test. They were both eager. These girls, Sara and Morgan, both believed they were good people, and were confident at taking the test. They actually asked me to go through all the Ten Commandments to see how they'd do. After going through them, they realized they were guilty of almost all of them.

Both the girls became very nervous and quiet. Morgan began nervously scratching her arm, and Sara looked down. Around this time, Sara's Mom walked up, and hearing the conversation, said she would be around for a few minutes, but then they had to leave. Unbeknownst to me, she then stood a few feet behind me, listening to most of the conversation. It's a good thing I didn't know she was there, because this is a fear of mine: talking to an adolescent or child, and a parent walks up and says something like, "Hey! You're brainwashing my kid! Leave my child alone, you creep!" (Although this has never happened to me before).

Anyway, the girls were very concerned and disturbed by their standing before God, and admitted they would go to Hell if they died tonight.

"What are you going to do about it?"

"Try to live a better life and keep the Ten Commandments."

I tried to explain to her that it is too late for that; she'd already broken them. "It's like saying, 'Yes, judge, I ran a red light, but I've gone through fifty green lights!' That wouldn't work before a judge, right? You'd still be guilty."

The girls agreed.

"Or what if some guy was found guilty of child-molesting, but his defense was that he had given lots of money to charity and washed the judge's car. The judge would say, 'That's great, and thanks, but that has nothing to do with your court case.' Right?" The girls agreed.

"You must repent and trust in Jesus."

They agreed.

"Do you want to do that now?" They looked at each other and agreed, nodding fervently, but solemnly.

"Okay, then pray that to God. You pray now and I'll pray for you. Do you want to do that?"

"You mean, out loud?"

"Yes. You don't have to do it if you don't want to. I don't want to push you into anything."

"No, we want to!"

So, feeling quite uncomfortable, Sara asked, "So what do we pray?"

"Tell God you repent—turn from your sins and toward God, and trust in Jesus."

They seemed quite uncomfortable with praying aloud with strangers, but went ahead with it nonetheless. I was encouraged that they prayed aloud because I wanted to know that they truly repented and trusted Jesus. I didn't want to lead these girls into a false conversion, and then assure them that their sins are forgiven. Then I prayed for them, thanking God for His forgiveness for them, and asking Him for guidance and wisdom for these girls as they seek to know Him and follow Him. After this, their mom appeared, smiling, and told the girls it was time to leave. They thanked us for our time and left.

I was stoked. As Sam and I walked back to the car, we approached another group of teens. After talking for a few minutes, one girl in particular was hit by the seriousness of her sins, and although her friends were walking off, she agreed that she had to get right with God that night.

Wow! One person after another was becoming a Christian or else desiring to do it that night. Sam and I walked back to the center of the Commons area and saw a few more kids, joking around. Several of them were standing up, and some were sitting on the curb. I gave them "Are You A Good Person?" booklets, and asked them if they wanted to take the Good Person Test. All of them declined except a girl named Nina. After talking for a few minutes, Nina became wide-eyed when she realized her state before God.

"Would you go to Heaven or Hell?" I asked her.

"Hell!" she said out of alarm and concern, so loud that the others started looking at her. This girl was serious.

"What?" a young woman's voice yelled. "He said you're going to Hell!?!" I looked up to see what looked like Nina's older sister, sitting on the curb. "Nina, come here now! No more tests!" At this moment, I began to feel like a creep. My fear was starting to come true.

"No!" Nina replied. "It's okay, it's okay!" Her sister insisted. Nina looked at me, still distressed. Great! Now what?

"God did something so you wouldn't have to go to Hell! Read that booklet!" I said to her quickly. She nodded in agreement as she quickly joined her older sister. Sam and I walked off. That encounter actually encouraged me. I saw Nina's sincerity. The Law had done its work. I can now only hope that she had a chance to look at the tract without her sister taking it away from her.

My afterthoughts about tonight: The only thing I did differently tonight than how I normally witness was that I was more confident and compassionate. I let others see compassion on my face, and spoke like, "Hey, you know this and I know this. Let's face it!" I didn't speak in a lofty way or abstractly, but very concretely, *expecting* that they would know just what I was talking about and understand.

1

Shutdown of Liberties

by Ray Comfort

A s you read the New Testament, you will find phrases such as "Satan hindered us." But at the same time, there is a tremendous optimism because God Himself fights with us, and if God is for us, nothing can be against us. The loss of any battle is no reason for discouragement when we have the knowledge that we eventually win the war.

On Friday, September 30, 2005, after daily preaching the gospel outside the local courthouse for more than two years, a judge shut us down. We were banned from public soil, even though we were preaching peacefully before the courts opened. A lengthy court case ensued.

In the meanwhile, we began daily preaching to crowds outside the local Department of Motor Vehicles—on public property, peacefully before the DMV opened. After three weeks, the police told us that we were an "event," and therefore needed a million-dollar insurance policy and a permit issued ten days before each event.

I was deeply concerned that moves were being made to ban "Intelligent Design" from being taught in schools. So I purchased a $4,000 gorilla suit, put one of our staff members into it, and preached the gospel outside the local high school. If they wouldn't let us talk about "Intelligent Design" inside schools, we would talk about it outside schools on public property. Hundreds of kids packed around to listen, but to my dismay, when teachers heard what I was saying, they walked through the crowd and kept repeating a very firm, "Go home!" The kids looked at me and said, "We have to go or we will be suspended," and the crowd dissipated.

So I took teams to local malls on Friday nights to share the gospel one-on-one. For two weeks in a row, I was kicked out of two different malls. Authorities in one mall said that I was "soliciting" by handing out tracts and speaking to people. The other was more blatant, saying that I wasn't allowed to speak to anyone "about God or Jesus" in the mall.

A few months earlier on Christmas Eve, I took a team and we sang carols, handed out tracts, and spoke about the true meaning of Christmas and gifts to children outside of a Wal-Mart. While we were singing, one of the managers opened the door and asked, "Do you have a permit to do this?" We didn't have a permit because a well-known court case had concluded that anyone had a right to set up a table outside of a Wal-Mart because it was a place of public access. When the manager asked that question, a woman in the crowd became very irate and said, "If you stop these people from singing Christmas carols, I will return what I have purchased from you and never shop here again." God bless her.

With God's help, I never want to say, "The world can go to Hell. I don't care." I do care, so the following week I went back to the mall, stayed away from security guards, kept moving, and gave out about 80 tracts. As one young man, with two huge earrings in his ears and various pieces metal in his face, stared at the Million Dollar Bill tract I had given him, I said, "It's a gospel tract. What do you think happens after someone dies?"

"They go to Heaven or to Hell."

"Where do you think that you will go?"

"To Heaven, I hope."

"So, you consider yourself to be a good person?"

"Yes. I'm a really good person."

"May I give you a quick four-question test to see if that's true?"

"I'm pretty pressed for time."

"I could walk along with you."

"Okay."

"Have you ever told a lie?"

"Yes."

"What does that make you?"

"A liar."

"Have you ever stolen anything?"

"No."

"Have you ever used God's name in vain?"

"Yes."

"That's called *blasphemy*. It's when you use God's name as a cuss word. It's a very serious crime in His sight. Jesus said, 'Whoever looks upon a woman to lust after her has committed adultery already with her in his heart.' Have you ever looked at a woman with lust?"

"Yes."

"What's your name?"

"Hector."

"Hector, by your own admission, you are a lying, blasphemous adulterer at heart. If God judges you by the Ten Commandments on the Day of Judgment, will you be innocent or guilty?"

"Guilty."

"Will you go to Heaven or Hell?"

"Hell."

"Does that concern you?"

"It *does* concern me."

I then shared the good news of the Cross, the resurrection, and his need of repentance and faith. "Do you have a Bible?"

His face went blank, and he said, "My girlfriend just gave me one!"

"Well, you can be sure she's praying for you, and I'm an answer to her prayers. So listen to what I have told you. Thanks for listening to me."

We shook hands and parted.

A few days later I was riding my bike home from work, when I rode past a young man who was leaning against a wall. As I did so I said, "How you doing?"

He answered, "What's up?"

I kept riding. He had asked me what's up and I had ignored him! The thought struck me that with God's help, the life of that man could be transformed. Just by stopping and telling him what was up, I could have a conversation with him that he would never forget. God could use my words to save him from Hell. I stopped my bike, turned it around, and rode back to him.

He seemed intrigued that I would suddenly come back, and as I put my hand in my pocket to get some tracts, he stepped toward me. Another youth, who was obviously his friend suddenly appeared. Both of them had friendly body language.

"Did you guys get one of these?"

As I left the ministry I had picked up two "Smart Cards" and put them in my pocket.

"Put your thumb on that 'box' and if you are a good person, it will turn a greenish blue."

Of course, after they both held their thumbs on the box for the required fourteen seconds; nothing happened.

"Do you think you are good people?"

"Kind of."

"Well, let's do a test. Have you ever told a lie?"

Their names were Mike and Alfredo, and both of them were lying, thieving, blasphemous adulterers at heart.

Mike said that he had been lusting that day, but when it came to Judgment Day, he said, "I won't be guilty because I have given myself to Jesus Christ."

Alfredo admitted his guilt and said that he would end up in Hell.

I turned to Mike and said, "There are three things that make me concerned for you. You just told me that you had been lusting. You can't call yourself a Christian and keep sinning. You are deceiving yourself. When did you last read your Bible?"

"To be honest, it's been quite some time."

"Also, you said that you are a good person, when the Bible says that there are none good. Plenty of people say that they have given their lives to Jesus, but that's not going to help them on Judgment Day. They have been hypocrites."

"Have you guys been drinking alcohol?"

"How'd you know?"

"You smell of alcohol. That gave me a clue."

They weren't drunk, but it strengthened my argument that Mike wasn't right with God. I then shared the gospel with them, and told them that they needed to truly repent. Then I pointed to our ministry, told them I wrote books, and said they were welcome to drop into our store and get a free book.

Alfredo said, "My girlfriend loves reading."

I looked at him and asked, "Have you been having sex out of marriage?"

"Yes."

"That's called fornication. You are in big trouble. Thanks, guys, for talking with me." We shook hands and I left, thanking God for the liberty I have to stop and share the gospel on the streets of our country.

Two days later, both Mike and Alfredo showed up in the lobby of our ministry. I gave them a tour, loaded them up with CDs, books, and New Testaments, and prayed with them before they left.

That night I took a team to Knott's Berry Farm, a huge theme park in Southern California, which is ten minutes from our ministry. The park was founded by a Christian family many years ago, and they even had a church service as part of the theme park until recently when, for some reason, it was moved across the road. The normally busy place was surprisingly very quiet, but we were able to hand out some tracts, which were well received, and I witnessed to four young people. But as we were leaving, a security guard approached three of our team members and said, "You are not allowed to talk about religion in this place. You will have to leave." The irony was that it was quiet, and our team was easily spotted because a Christian denomination had rented the entire park, and it was shut to the public.

What do you do when your liberties are taken from you? I have learned that you don't take what liberties you have left for granted. You are like a man who has always eaten meals without a second thought. But when a famine strikes, he then bows his head and thanks God for every bite.

Losing liberties has made me take advantage of liberties. It has made me more resolute to make bold approaches to sinners, and I am thankful for every person to whom I witness. It's made me say with Winston Churchill when the Nazis took Europe and threatened to conquer his homeland, "We will fight on the beaches. We will fight on the shores. We will *never* surrender."

John Wesley once conducted an experiment that is extremely interesting. It was June 8, 1740. He said,

"For these two days I had made an experiment which I had so often and earnestly been pressed to do— speaking to none concerning the things of God unless my heart was free to it."[13]

In other words, he decided not to witness unless he *felt* like doing it. He then related the result of this experiment. He said that (1) he rode in a horse-drawn carriage for eighty miles without witnessing to a soul, except for a few superficial words of greeting; (2) he had no cross to bear or take up (he didn't feel like a "religious weirdo") and he fell asleep for two hours; and (3) he had much respect shown to him, and was considered "a civil, good-natured gentleman."

Then he lamented, "Oh, how pleasing is all this to flesh and blood! Need ye 'compass sea and land' to make 'proselytes' to this?" In other words, using the words of Jesus when He called a particular convert "a child of Hell"[14]—is this what we are supposed to be?

If we care about the unsaved, we must *make* ourselves speak to them. If we go by our "feelings," we will always take the low road of the world's approval. To witness for Christ means a continual denial of self, of comfort, and of wanting worldly respect. It means bearing the reproach of the Cross. Charles Spurgeon so rightly said, "We must school and train ourselves to deal personally with the unconverted. We must not excuse ourselves, but force ourselves to the irksome task until it becomes easy." And even when we become so adept that sharing the gospel is second nature, we can never wait until we *feel* like it. That never happens. No sane firefighter waits for his feelings to tell him to brave the flames. His feelings tell him that he could get horribly burned. He risks his life to rescue victims because of his continual resolute firefighting mindset.

The Million Dollar Machine

After Kirk got his chickens, I was flooded with joy-filled memories of collecting fresh eggs back in New Zealand before we moved to the States. After some reasoning with my loving wife, we now have five chickens. I love them, and I've even give them their own names: Crispy, Tender, Finger-lickin,

Original, and Roast. I printed their names out and put them on the wall of their coop to help them to remember why they were part of our happy family.

Chickens remind me of myself. Whenever I have someone turn down a tract, the tenderness of my flesh becomes very evident. Rejection cuts to the bone. But I have found that there is something I can do about my tenderness. I get into the mindset of being a pre-programmed machine. I say to myself, "I am a machine. I am pre-programmed to have a love and concern for the lost. Fear has no part of me. Rejection bounces off me. I am a machine."

After the Secret Service seized our Million Dollar Bill tract in Texas early in June of 2006 and then took a supply from a quadriplegic as he passed them out in Las Vegas, my appreciation deepened for the fact that the tract had helped me to be like a machine. Our ministry has about seventy different tracts, but for me the Million Dollar Bill is number one, and the thought of losing my first love made my heart grow fonder. So I decided to have one enlarged and put on the wall of our ministry as a kind of trophy or (if the Secret Police had their way) a fond memorial.

As I walked though the store, I handed them to different people who were standing by printers and computers. No rejections. Not one. As usual, the recipients looked startled for a moment, then laughed and made jokes about how they could now quit work.

As I stood at the counter two females (in their early 20s) lined up behind me. I was pre-programmed. I turned around and with a friendly voice said,

"Hello. Did you get your million?"

"Huh?"

"It's a million dollars. It's great when you get the change."

"Thanks!"

I followed up with a "Department of Annoyance" card for each of them and said, "This is where I'm from—the Department of Annoyance."

One of them laughed. The other for some reason handed the card to her friend and clutched her million. So I gave her a "Smart Card" and said, "Don't give this one away."

She looked at it and said, "I *am* a good person."

"There's a four-question test you can take to see if that's true. Let's do it. Have you ever told a lie?"

"Yes."

"What does that make you?"

"A liar."

"Have you ever stolen something?"

"No. Never."

She had used God's name in vain, but she maintained that she had never lusted. Not once.

"You've never looked at a guy with sexual desire, with lust? You have a pure heart?"

Suddenly another woman arrived at the counter and asked, "Whatcha talking about?"

I handed her a bill.

Miss Pureheart said, "Lust. You know, when you look at a guy and you know..."

It turned out that she *had* lusted for her boyfriend before they got together and that she went to church, but wasn't born again. I told her to read the rest of the tract.

I then noticed that three more women were standing behind me. One of them was staring at me so I gave her my last Million Dollar Bill, and apologized to her friend that she didn't get one. She gave an understanding smile.

Then the lady in front of her indignantly asked, "How come you passed me by?"

I apologized to her also and told her that there had been a run on the bank, but that there was a reserve supply in my van.

I turned back to the counter and placed the order for the banner for my favorite tract.

Behind me I could hear the woman who had the bill begin reading it out loud—"Have you ever told a lie, stolen anything, or used God's name in vain?"

Then a heated discussion began.

"You do that!"

"No, I don't!"

"Yes, you do."

"I do not use God's name in vain!"

"You do! All the time."

"Okay then, so do you!"

I smiled as I listened to them, then finished ordering the banner and went out to my van.

Suddenly there was a loud honk. It was Mrs. Indignant. *She wanted her Million Dollar Bill!* I grabbed three or four and a "What Hollywood Believes" CD and handed them to her through her car window. She was ecstatic.

When our lawyers were preparing a deposition against the Federal Government for seizing private property without a warrant, they asked me how many copies of the tract I had personally given out. I gave a conservative estimate that to that point it was around 30,000. It was then that I realized *how much* this little tract had helped me conquer my fears. It took *millions* to change me from a chicken into a machine. So I'm going to hold onto my millions like a stubborn rich man in an unarmed robbery, and if the Federal Government does take them from me, they're going to have a fight on their hands, God-willing, right up to the Supreme Court.

In Conclusion

It was a very cold Monday morning (for Southern California) in March of 2006. I turned on the television set at 5:00 a.m. to see the weather forecast, and as usual did a quick channel-surf before I braved getting out of bed. I stopped on "Zola," a Christian television program on prophecy by Zola Levitt. I had met Zola a few years earlier while I was in Jerusalem, found him to be a very nice man, and enjoyed his program. He began this day with an awkward, "There's no other way to say this ... um ... I've contracted lung cancer. I'm very sick ... probably I'll see the Lord this year, I suppose. That's what the forecast is ..." It was a sobering moment.

Then he said, "I expect that as time goes on, my voice will weaken. One thing this cancer does is pull out the vocal cords. It's already weakened, so I wanted to talk to you right away about some things I wanted to say. Not that I am the expert or anything, but you are my people that watch our program and I wanted to tell you some things. First off—witness ... *everyone*. Get out there and witness *all the time!*"[15]

I had seen his television program many times and it was usually about prophecy and worshipping God. How remarkable! Here was a man who knew he was going to die. He was losing his voice. He had no doubt been thinking about what he wanted to say to his viewers. What was most important? *It was to share the gospel.* His words reminded me of the last thing Jesus said before He departed from this earth: "Go into all the world and preach the gospel to every creature. You are my witnesses." He said to "Go out and witness."

So, please, go out and witness. Share the gospel because it's an adventure to do so. Share it because there's nothing better to do with your time. Witness while you have the liberty to do so. Do it while you have a voice. Do it because sinners are going to Hell. Do it because you have been commanded to. Do it because of the Cross.

Footnotes

1 See www.WayoftheMaster.com.

2 See Million Dollar Bill tract at www.WayoftheMaster.com.

3 See "The Light Show" at www.WayoftheMaster.com.

4 Agape Press (June 3, 2005).

5 After reading this article, a tender Christian woman wrote and accused Kirk of being deceitful. I responded and explained that Kirk was "tongue in cheek" with this incident, and that he would never deceive his wife. We are close friends, and I can testify that he has such high integrity, it would shame the average Christian. – Ray Comfort.

6 Larry's wife.

7 A reference to the "Hell's Best Kept Secret" teaching.

8 Available through www.wayofthemaster.com.

9 Bridge-Logos Publishers.

10 The Basic Training Course (www.WayoftheMaster.com).

11 Available through www.WayoftheMaster.com.

12 See www.thegreatnews.com.

13 *The Journal of John Wesley*, Moody Press, edited by Percy Livingstone Parker, p. 90.

14 Matthew 23:15.

15 Zola died a few months later.

OTHER BOOKS BY RAY COMFORT

The Way of the Master Evidence Bible: Pocket NT,
   Psalms and Proverbs (leather & paperback)
The Way of the Master Evidence Bible: Old and
   New Testaments: paperback, hardback, leather:
   burgundy and black
The School of Biblical Evangelism (Ray Comfort and
   Kirk Cameron)
How to Win Souls and Influence People
God Doesn't Believe in Atheists
101 Things Husbands Do to Annoy Their Wives
Nostradamus: Attack on America
Scientific Facts in the Bible
What Did Jesus Do?
What Hollywood Believes (Genesis Publishing Group)
Miracle in the Making
*How to Bring Your Children to Christ and
   Keep Them There* (Genesis Publishing Group)
Life's Emergency Handbook (Ray Comfort and
   Kirk Cameron)
Out of the Comfort Zone
Hell's Best Kept Secret (Whitaker House)
Spurgeon Gold
Whitefield Gold
Overcoming Panic Attacks
The Way of the Master Minute (Ray Comfort and
   Kirk Cameron)
How to Live Forever Without Being Religious
Intelligent Design Vs. Evolution: Letters to An Atheist
The Way of the Master
The Way of the Master for Kids (Ray Comfort and
   Kirk Cameron)

The Dr. Zilch Series

Eight books that have nothing to say:

- *Scientific Proof for Evolution*
- *Everything Man Has Learned About Women*
- *What Science Can Do to Stop the Aging Process*
- *How to Be Rich Beyond Your Wildest Dreams and what you can do to make sure you will* always *have it*
- *What Man Has Learned From History*
- *Evidence for Atheism*
- *What You Can Do to Go to Heaven*
- *What Religion Can Do for You*

At first glance it would seem that these books have nothing to say, but even though every one of their 160 pages is blank, the silence of *nothing* speaks volumes for the reader. The back cover then presents a discrete but uncompromising gospel message written by Ray Comfort. Think of those people you care about who don't know the Lord. Where will they go if they die today? *Don't wait any longer.* Give them one of these unique publications. It may cause them to smile, and at the same time consider closely life's most important issue.

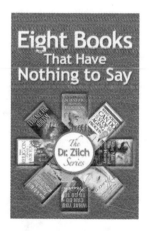

Basic Training Course

Ray Comfort and Kirk Cameron especially created "The Basic Training Course" for use in the local church. Based on the award-winning TV series, "The Way of the Master," this dynamic eight-session course will equip groups and individuals to simply and confidently share the gospel with family, friends, and strangers.

Learn to bypass the intellect (the place of argument) and speak directly to the conscience (the place of the knowledge of right and wrong)—the way Jesus did. Kirk and Ray will motivate you, help you conquer your fears, and will not only explain how to share the gospel biblically but will demonstrate it. Watch as they witness to gang members, atheists, cult members, intellectuals, Jews, on the beach, in parks, on planes, and in malls.

Includes 4 DVDs, audio CDs, Study Guide, Quick Reference Card, and 300 Icebreakers (tracts) to help you get your feet wet.

The course is commended by John MacArthur, Ravi Zacharias, and Josh McDowell.

See www.WayoftheMaster.com for details, or call 1(800) 437-1893

DON'T MISS

Springboards for Budding Preachers
(comes with six DVDs)
Twenty-eight live open-air gospel messages by Ray Comfort

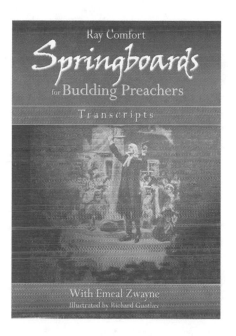

For more than two and a half years, Ray Comfort and Emeal Zwayne (General Manager of The Way of the Master and Living Waters Publications) preached the gospel open-air to the crowds waiting daily outside the courtroom in Bellflower, California. During that time, an estimated 30,000 people heard the gospel.

On September 30, 2005, a Los Angeles County judge issued a court order forbidding public speaking, affecting not only this court, but the grounds of more than forty courtrooms in L.A. County, despite the fact that it is public soil. Fortunately, our sound man, Stuart Scott, recorded the last 28 days of the preaching. These messages are packed with illustrations and springboards for open-air preachers, so you can learn how to speak boldly while we still have opportunity.

Make sure you tune into The Way of the Master Radio
(with Todd Friel, Ray Comfort and Kirk Cameron:
www.WayoftheMasterRadio.com

* * *

I have one complaint about the radio show. Since I began
listening, I can't listen to anything else in my truck. I'm addicted!
I need a 12-step program to get off. My wife gave me an
ultimatum. She said either the WOTM goes or she goes. Man,
I'm going to miss her! – F. Sankey (PA).

* * *

A little more than a week ago my life was turned upside down
after listening to *Hell's Best Kept Secret* and *True and False
Conversions*. I realized that I was not in the faith and had not
truly repented. I was almost in a car accident recently and
thought I would go to Heaven. Thank you for the TRUTH!
Now I am so concerned about everyone who is like I was. I
have since repented and even used your method of witnessing
on, of all people, my ex-husband. I watched his eyes fill up
with tears, and though I did not pray with him right there, he
has begun attending church. I did this right after he did not
buy the "God has a plan for an abundant life" altar call at my
church. He is very smart and did not buy that. I went over the
Commandments with him, told the parachute story, and then I
could see that need for Jesus in his face. It was awesome! God
bless you all! – Tracy R.

* * *

Listen to *Hell's Best Kept Secret* and *True and False
Conversion* freely online at www.LivingWaters.com